BECOMING
A PARISH OF
INTENTIONAL
DISCIPLES

BECOMING
A PARISH OF
INTENTIONAL
DISCIPLES

SHERRY A. WEDDELL,
EDITOR

OUR SUNDAY VISITOR PUBLISHING DIVISION
OUR SUNDAY VISITOR, INC.
HUNTINGTON, INDIANA 46750

20 19 18 17 16 15   1 2 3 4 5 6 7 8 9

ISBN: 978-1-61278-834-0 (Inventory No. T1641)
eISBN: 978-1-61278-379-6
LCCN: 2014955267

Cover design: Lindsey Riesen
Cover art: iStockphoto
Interior design: Dianne Nelson

PRINTED IN THE UNITED STATES OF AMERICA

CONTENTS

ACKNOWLEDGMENTS

Unless otherwise noted, Scripture texts in this work are taken from the *New American Bible, revised edition* © 2010, 1991, 1986, 1970 Confraternity of Christian Doctrine, Washington, D.C., and are used by permission of the copyright owner. All rights reserved. No part of the *New American Bible* may be reproduced in any form without permission in writing from the copyright owner.

Where noted, other Scripture texts are from the *Revised Standard Version of the Bible — Second Catholic Edition* (RSV), copyright © 2006 National Council of the Churches of Christ in the United States of America. Used by permission. All rights reserved.

Quotations from papal and other Vatican-generated documents available on vatican.va are copyright © 2015 by Libreria Editrice Vaticana.

English translation of the *Catechism of the Catholic Church* for use in the United States of America copyright © 1994, United States Catholic Conference, Inc. — Libreria Editrice Vaticana. English translation of the *Catechism of the Catholic Church: Modifications from the Editio Typica* copyright © 1997, United States Catholic Conference, Inc. — Libreria Editrice Vaticana.

NOTE TO THE READER

During the first fifteen years of the Catherine of Siena Institute's ministry, I often told people that we worked "in the grassiest of the grass roots." (How grassy? Let's just say I've driven thousands of miles to workshops across landscapes so flat and so empty that a cow lying down a quarter-mile away is a major landmark.) Over the years, our network of teachers and facilitators has worked with tens of thousands of Catholics in the pews and many thousands of clerical and lay leaders in well over 500 parishes, from the smallest and most rural to the largest congregations in the United States and in eleven other countries.

It was at this most basic level of the Church's life that I slowly became aware that there was a whole unsung army of evangelizers that Catholics never talked about. Some were just beginning to explore the idea of making disciples, and others were highly gifted evangelical geniuses whose vision and efforts were already changing individual lives, whole parishes, and — occasionally — whole dioceses. None of these evangelizers were publishing books or speaking at national conferences — yet. Their names and their work were only recognized locally, and sometimes they were not known or honored even there.

To witness and to be able to share in this powerful ministry of apostolic grace in action at the parish level has been an abiding source of joy and hope for me. That's why I asked some of these amazing evangelizing practitioners to share their experiences and insights with the larger Church in this book. The majority have worked as Institute teachers for years, in addition to their parochial ministries, and it has been an honor to have them as part of our CSI team and to learn from them. I hope that reading *Becoming a Parish of Intentional Disciples* will be as inspiring and challenging for you as knowing and collaborating with these intentional disciples and disciple-makers has been for me.

Sherry A. Weddell

CHAPTER ONE

The Generation of Saints

Sherry A. Weddell

On September 14, 1594, a newly ordained priest named Francis de Sales set out on foot — with a single companion — to re-evangelize the 60,000 formerly Catholic inhabitants of a region called the Chablais in alpine France. De Sales described the situation on the ground:

> When we entered those bailiwicks, sad indeed did everything appear. For we saw sixty-five parishes, in which, except the officials of the Duke, there were not, among so many thousands of persons, one hundred Catholics. The Churches, partly stripped, partly in ruins; nowhere the sign of the cross, nowhere altars; and everywhere all vestiges of the ancient and true faith destroyed....[1]

Four years later, a spectacular, public Forty Hours of Eucharistic Adoration was held in the Chablais' capital city of Thonon. Forty thousand citizens of the Chablais had become Catholic in only four years largely because of the tireless personal apostolate of a single man.

---

[1] Rev. H.B. Mackey, O.S.B., *S. Francis de Sales, Doctor of the Church* (London: Burns & Oates, 1883), p. 12.

Francis de Sales' remarkable mission to the Chablais was not only the dramatic beginning of his own priestly life, but it also marked the beginning of a great Catholic revival in France that affected the course of that country for 150 years. Francis became the seminal father figure in a multi-generational French network of disciple-friends, whom historian Orest Ranum named "the Generation of Saints":

> Though of not quite the same age group, they were all intimately acquainted and, more important, were inspired to become more holy and zealous from personal contact with each other. They visited one another frequently or kept up active correspondence about their visions, prayers, sense of sin, and missionary activities. In a way, they set out as a group to remake the Church....[2]

Some historians regard the revival as lasting only between 1600 and 1640. I would argue that we should include the entire sixty-six years from the beginning of Francis de Sales' mission to the Chablais through 1660, when St. Vincent de Paul died. Many of the prime movers and shakers are familiar names today: Sts. Francis de Sales, Vincent de Paul, Jane de Chantal, and Louise de Marillac. Some who were hugely influential in their day are hardly known at all now.

THE UNEXPECTED PARIS

As a group, they were remarkable for their diversity. Thousands were actively involved in the renewal, but the major figures

---

[2] Orest Ranum, *Paris in the Age of Absolutism: An Essay* (University Park, PA: Pennsylvania State University Press, 2002), p. 172.

included a cardinal, a bishop, three priests (including one who had grown up a peasant and spent time as a slave), two young widows with children, a Parisian housewife, a single woman, a professional soldier, and a shoemaker. Today, the same group is recognized for including four canonized saints, two blesseds, one Doctor of the Church, and six founders of religious congregations.

A historian friend told me that to understand the significance of the revival, I first needed to research the very dark days that set the stage for emergence of the generation of saints. It was certainly eye opening. The history of France between 1560 and 1600 reads like an endless litany of religious civil wars, massacres, sieges, famine, a reign of terror, and some of the nastiest diatribes ever written.

As I did my research, I began to realize that I had a powerful, unspoken image of Paris, nurtured by innumerable films. The Myth-That-Is-Paris runs like this: When Americans want to get out from under our bourgeois, work-obsessed, joyless Puritanism; when we want to discover our inner passion, artist, and cool, we go where an irresistible tide will carry us away — guiltless — and tutor us in the art of living. We — like Audrey Hepburn, Anne Hathaway, and Gene Kelly — go to Paris, our personal, religion-free paradise.

But the historical reality is very different — and not always edifying. For at least fifty years, Paris was not only the largest city in Europe but also one of the most religious cities on earth. Paris in 1590 could easily give Protestant Geneva and sixteenth-century Spain a run for their money in a contest for most uber-religious culture in history.

Paris was *the* center of Catholic resistance in the Wars of Religion between Catholics and Protestants. For six years in the 1590s, Paris was run by the ultra-Catholic Holy League. Penitential Eucharistic processions filled the streets of the capital for months at a time. The more-Catholic-than-thou

Holy League was known to arrest citizens at Mass for not being Catholic enough.

Parisians endured months of siege and starvation and watched 20 percent of the city's population die rather than accept a Protestant king. It was the intransigence of Parisian Catholics that ultimately forced the Protestant heir to the French throne, Henry of Navarre, to become the Catholic King Henry IV. (Henry IV never said, "Paris is worth a Mass." The quip that launched a thousand bad histories was coined by ultra-Catholic propagandists who insisted that Henry was not capable of conversion.)

When a tentative peace was restored under the convert king and the Edict of Nantes (1598), the new stability included a reality that was completely unprecedented: a permanent Protestant minority.

But Paris was also the center of the great Catholic revival that followed the conflict and which transformed France. It is essential that we grasp that while the civil conflict was the *occasion* of the revival, it did not *cause* the revival. The reform-minded Catholics saw the emergence of Protestantism not as the *cause* of all of France's problems, but as a *symptom*. It was when the reformers began to consider their own sins and failures as well as the failures of the larger French Church that things began to change. It was when they turned to prayer, penance, and a life of serious, communal devotion and mission (seventeenth-century language for "intentional discipleship") that the revival began.

What Love Will Do

The Catholic Revival in France regained much of the ground that had been lost because it produced a tidal wave of spiritual, evangelical, and pastoral reforms and innovations. The reform began well before the decrees of the Council of Trent were finally published in France in 1615, more than fifty years after the council had ended. The reformers were not attempting to restore the pre-Reformation Church, which they knew was gone beyond recall. What they did do was re-invent Catholic life, practice, and spirituality in an evangelical mode. They not only birthed new initiatives themselves, but they also imported and built upon innovations from other parts of Catholic Europe, such as the Carmel of Teresa of Ávila in Spain, the Oratory of Philip Neri in Rome, and the Confraternity of Catholic Doctrine in Milan.

It was providential that the central personality of the first generation of saints was St. Francis de Sales, whose gentleness and trust in God were proverbial. "Let us see what love will do" was his motto. It was De Sales' influence that meant that while the generation that lived through the wars was marked for life, the next generation could turn their energies to heroic, systematic charity, evangelization, and missionary expansion; systematic Catholic education and catechesis; the renewal of the priesthood, the parish, and religious life; and establishing the seminary system.

Heroic love birthed a vast spectrum of apostolic creativity and transformation and gave rise to most of the institutions that American Catholics now regard as completely traditional.

The revival was deeply influenced by what is often called the "French School" of spirituality, although St. Vincent de Paul followed a somewhat different path. The French School, as it existed in the seventeenth century, was not a system or philosophy but a highly Christocentric approach to Catholic faith, characterized by a sense of adoration, a personal relationship with Jesus, and a rediscovery of the Holy Spirit. The great figures of the French School — Cardinal Pierre Berulle, Father

Jean-Jacques Olier, the mystic Charles de Condren, and St. John Eudes — focused intensely on the Incarnate Son of God in a way that struck their contemporaries as new and even controversial because such a profoundly Christocentric Catholicism had not been seen in France since the High Middle Ages. It was said of St. John Eudes:

> The challenge facing this pastor's heart was to help each Christian discover the riches of his/her Baptism. The idea he proposes to every baptized person is to "FORM, SANCTIFY, ALLOW JESUS TO LIVE AND REIGN IN US."[3]

The discussions at the Second Vatican Council drew upon key spiritual principles that had inspired the French School 300 years earlier. One was the universal call of all Christians to holiness; a deep understanding that all laypeople, women and men religious, priests and deacons were called to personal union with Jesus at the heart of the Church and to apostolic witnessing. Francis de Sales wrote the first great Catholic work on a truly lay spirituality, *Introduction to the Devout Life*, which had a huge impact on French Catholics and fueled a new respect for and openness to collaborating in mission with the laity. And the fruit of that collaboration was incredible.

WIVES, WIDOWS, SHOEMAKERS

Barbe Acarie was a standout example of the kind of lay leadership that was widespread in the generation of saints. Barbe, whose nickname was "La Belle Acarie," was a wife, mother, and mystic

---

[3] The Eudists of the Philippines, St. John Eudes and Pierre Berulle, http://www.eudistsphilippines.com/french-school-of-spirituality.html.

with great organizational gifts who had lived through the siege of Paris. For fifteen years, Barbe's Paris home served as a salon and meeting place for all the major leaders of the renewal. Teresa of Ávila, who had died years before, appeared to Barbe in a vision and asked her to bring the Discalced Carmelites to France. After discerning the validity of the vision with a group of reformers, including Francis de Sales, Barbe not only served as contractor for the building of the Carmelite convent but recruited, interviewed, and helped form the first group of novices.

An intimate friend described Barbe this way:

> She was responsible for at least 10,000 conversions. "All who approached her were impressed by her genuine spirituality, and felt that in talking with her they were coming very close to God Himself." Therefore, she "liberated grace" in countless men and women, including many priests.[4]

The collaboration of Gaston Jean Baptiste, Baron of Renty, and shoemaker Henry Michael Buch also tells us a great deal about the rich apostolic creativity of the movement. The Baron of Renty was a wealthy disciple-philanthropist who played multiple leadership roles in the renewal, but Henry Michael Buch hailed from a very different social class. He was the son of poor day-laborers and had been effectively evangelizing and forming many of his fellow shoemakers for years. The "Good Henry," as he was commonly known, was forty-five years old when the Baron of Renty first heard of him and asked to meet him.

---

[4] "Saint of the Day," St. Patrick Catholic Church, Blessed Mary of the Incarnation (also known as Madame Barbe Acarie), http://www.saintpatrickdc .org/ss/0430.shtml.

The Baron was so impressed by the spiritual depth of this simple workingman that he proposed that Henry found a confraternity of shoemakers and tailors, the Frères Cordonniers ("Brother Shoemakers"). Members of the confraternity would approach their trade as disciples and apostles, evangelize their coworkers, share their earnings with the poor, and live a common spiritual life according to an informal rule. The Baron paid for Henry to become a "master" of his trade, enabling him to take on apprentices and journeymen who were open to living lives of devotion. The confraternity eventually spread around France and Italy.

All of the disciple-friends driving the French renewal had a clear expectation that the Holy Spirit was at work, and there are many well-documented instances of divine inspiration setting the stage for fruitful collaboration. For instance, Jane de Chantal had a vision of a then-unknown bishop to whom she could entrust her spiritual life, while Francis de Sales had seen the image of a young widow in a vision. When the bishop and the widow finally met in 1604, both immediately recognized one another as the person God had prepared them to meet through their visions. This divine appointment was the springboard for their famously deep spiritual friendship. That friendship also led to the foundation of the Visitation Sisters — an innovative religious community for women who had a genuine call to religious life but were not strong enough to live the traditional life of rigorous austerity.

RELIGIOUS ORDERS, PARISH LIFE

The Visitation Sisters turned out to be just the tip of the religious-order iceberg. Seventy new religious houses were founded in Paris alone by 1650: forty-six new communities for woman and twenty-four communities for men. The majority of these new religious were contemplatives who lived ascetic lives. French monasticism enjoyed a great expansion and provided a real source of leadership and unity as well as a wellspring of prayer and penance in support of the revival.

The experience of Agnes Galand, now known as Blessed Agnes of Jesus, O.P., gives us a vivid sense of how the fruit of intercessory prayer could affect the course of the renewal. Agnes was an enclosed nun of the Dominican Order who experienced a vision in 1631 in which the Blessed Virgin Mary urged her to pray for an unknown priest with the command, "Pray to my Son for the Abbé of Prébrac."

Monsignor Jean-Jacques Olier happened to be that *abbé*, and while at a retreat led by St. Vincent de Paul he experienced a vision in which Mother Agnes appeared to him, though he had never met her. He later sought her out. When they met, she told him: "I have received orders from the Holy Virgin to pray for you. God has destined you to open the first seminaries in France."[5]

Jean-Jacques Olier's immense contributions to the renewal of French Catholicism had been foretold by Francis de Sales, who knew Olier's parents and predicted his role when Olier was only fourteen years old. His chance finally came in 1641. Olier and two other priests had begun living in community in Paris. Others soon joined them, and before long there were eight seminarians who lived with the priests, followed the same rule of life, and were being formed by Olier. The pastor of the local parish, encouraged by the presence of these zealous priests and seminarians, took a long vacation, during which time they reformed his parish.

---

5   "Bl. Agnes of Jesus of Langeac," Dominican Nuns of Summit, NJ (October 20, 2009, retrieved January 11, 2011), in http://en.wikipedia.org/wiki /Agnes_of_Jesus.

Word of the parish's transformation quickly spread and reached the ears of the overwhelmed pastor of St. Sulpice. His parish was not only the largest parish in France but was also commonly thought to be the most corrupt parish in all of Christendom. The pastor was inspired to offer his parish to Olier. And so in August 1641, Monsignor Olier took charge of St. Sulpice, whose territory included the left bank of the Seine and the University of Paris (Sorbonne). His modest aims were to reform this immense parish, establish a model seminary within the parish, and evangelize the Sorbonne. He had ten and a half years in which to do so before a stroke cut short his active ministry.

From the beginning, Olier looked outward, seeing both the whole person and the whole parish. He established thirteen catechetical centers scattered throughout the parish for both children and adults. Special formation was provided for every significant group, including beggars, domestic servants, midwives, workingmen, the elderly, and Protestants — hundreds of whom converted. Parishioners distributed pamphlets, holy pictures, and prayer books to those who did not come to church, and they also opened a bookstore at St. Sulpice.

The parish cared for the poor according to the methods inspired by Vincent de Paul and made free legal aid available. Orphans were taken in, and a number of free schools for poor girls were founded. St. Sulpice also housed nuns who had been driven out of their monasteries in the country by civil war. Olier worked tirelessly to overcome the common idea that a life of great devotion was only for priests and religious, and he inspired many around him to begin practicing the disciplines of discipleship.

In 1645, Olier founded the seminary of St. Sulpice nearby. A community of diocesan priests dedicated to the formation of clergy — the Sulpicians — grew out of the seminary. Olier desired that both his parish and the seminary serve as models that would help renew the diocesan priesthood. The seminary existed in great poverty for years, but within two years students had come from twenty different dioceses. Seminarians living at St. Sulpice were heavily involved in the remarkable ministries at the parish. Over time, St. Sulpice not only sent apostolically minded priests to every corner of France but became the model upon which seminaries were founded throughout the country.

THE MISSIONARY IMPERATIVE

As focused as Olier was on the needs of France, he, like many other leaders of the French revival, also had a strong interest in global missions, which produced remarkable fruit. In 1630, thirty-two-year-old Jérôme le Royer de la Dauversière attended Mass in Paris with his wife and three young children. While making his thanksgiving, Jérôme had a vision in which he felt called to found a congregation of women religious dedicated to caring for the "sick poor." Later he realized that God was also calling him to additional missionary work, including undertaking the colonization and evangelization of the island of Montreal in New France (now Canada).

La Dauversière shared his vision with Jean-Jacques Olier. Despite the fact that there were only about one hundred colonists scattered among a few primitive settlements in the whole of New France at the time, Olier took La Dauversière seriously. Together, Olier and Jérôme spread the vision, recruited settlers, and raised the money necessary to send a group of forty-five settlers to found a settlement on the island that would be a center of evangelization for the native peoples in the new world. They could not have known that they were also founding one of the great cities of the world.

Paul de Chomedey, a gifted and devout young soldier and leader, was appointed governor of the infant colony. Jeanne Mance, a single young woman who had discerned a missionary call, was also part of the original settlers. On May 18, 1642, the pioneers set foot on the Island of Montreal and celebrated Mass for the first time. The Blessed Sacrament remained exposed all day, with a vial containing fireflies as a sanctuary lamp.[6]

A year later, La Dauversière published a book on Ville-Marie, *The Purpose of Montreal*. He described the settlement one year after its founding: "The inhabitants live for the most part communally, as in a sort of inn; others live on their private means, but all live in Jesus Christ, with one heart and soul."[7]

That same year, Jeanne Mance founded the first hospital in Montreal, which she would run for many years. In 1655, she fell on ice, badly injuring her arm and losing its use. Jeanne sought healing three years later when she returned to Paris on colony business. In the chapel of St. Sulpice, she placed a relic of the late Father Jean-Jacques Olier's heart on her injured arm, and it was completely restored.

Jeanne Mance was not the only Catholic woman discerning a missionary call in seventeenth-century France. The French revival marked the beginning of the formal missionary apostolate of women in the Roman Catholic Church. One of the great catalysts for a widespread involvement in missions was the *Relations*, published by the French Jesuits every year from 1632 to 1673. The *Relations* narrated the most important events that had occurred in the past year in the Jesuit Canadian missions, and the reading of these reports aroused in the monasteries, religious institutions, and the devout laity of France a vast

---

6   *The Catholic Encyclopedia*, Volume 16, www.ccel.org.
7   Paul de Chomedey de Maisonneuve, CCHeritage.ca, http://www.ccheritage
     .ca/biographies/paulmaisonneuve.

movement of sympathy, prayers, and devotion in support of the missions in Canada.

When the Ursulines and Hospitallers, answering the appeal of the *Relations*, arrived at Quebec in 1639, it marked the first time that cloistered nuns had crossed the seas to carry out an apostolic mission. A number of other outstanding women missionaries were also drawn to serve in New France because of the *Relations*. "This participation of women in evangelization is a creation of Catholic and French origin, and it is what gives the colonization of Canada its true originality."[8]

The missionary zeal of seventeenth-century French Catholics was not limited to Canada. In 1659, intense French interest in missionary work resulted in the founding of the Society of Foreign Missions of Paris (Société des Missions Etrangères de Paris). The society was something really new, not a religious congregation but an organization of *secular priests and laypeople dedicated to missionary work in foreign countries*. In the 350 years since its founding, the society has sent out 4,200 missionary priests to Asia and North America.

THE HEART OF A SAINT

I cannot finish this very brief description of the generation of saints without a few paragraphs on the great St. Vincent de Paul. De Paul began life in a poor peasant family and grew up working the fields. As a young priest, he was ambitious for clerical advancement, reportedly was captured by Muslim pirates, served as a slave in North Africa, and eventually, back in

---

8   *Dictionary of Canadian Biography*, "Le Jeune, Paul," Léon Pouliot (University of Toronto/Université Laval, 1966-2014), http://www.biographi.ca/en/bio /le_jeune_paul_1E.html.

France, came under the influence of the French renewal. There he developed an intense commitment to the poor and oppressed. De Paul never lost his burning conviction that leaving private devotions for the sake of hands-on service of the poor, when called upon, was "leaving God for God."

His influence and leadership among the second generation of renewal leaders is impossible to overestimate. The reform and formation of the clergy, the evangelization of rural France, as well as systematic care for the sick, the destitute, the imprisoned, the refugees, and those suffering at every level were all transformed by his sustained concern.

The year 1625 was a major turning point for De Paul and for the Catholic Church in France. It was the year that he founded the Congregation of the Mission (Vincentians), a community of priests dedicated to holding month-long missions in rural parishes. (Although France had been Catholic for a thousand years, Vincent de Paul realized that huge portions of the countryside had never been evangelized and that the quality of pastoral care available in the countryside often ranged from poor to nonexistent.)

In an attempt to address the miserable level of formation among diocesan clergy, Vincent also began offering ten-day formation retreats for priests. In 1633, he started the famous *conférences des mardi*, Tuesday-afternoon gatherings of ordained and near-ordained clerics who met at the Vincentian center, Saint-Lazare, for ongoing spiritual and priestly formation. Two hundred fifty priests — many of whom became reformers themselves — participated in the Tuesday conferences during de Paul's lifetime. While admitting that De Paul "did not inaugurate a movement destined to end in the regeneration and organization of the clergy," respected biographer Pierre Coste concludes that "he was, in the hands of God, the instrument that most powerfully contributed to its success."[9]

The year 1625 was also the period when Louise de Marillac become a widow and met "Monseigneur Vincent" (as his friends called him), beginning a personal collaboration that lasted until their deaths. De Paul had started local parish-based "Charities" that were devotional confraternities run by laywomen and focused on the practice of the works of mercy. He wanted to establish Charities in every parish in which his congregation held a mission — to sustain and consolidate the spiritual impact of the mission.

Louise de Marillac began by visiting, reviving, and forming the members of existing parish Charities, but her vision grew as she did. In time, Louise and some of her collaborators felt called to form a new kind of active religious community dedicated to a comprehensive, hands-on service of the poor; a community that would not take solemn vows or be enclosed: the Daughters of Charity.

St. Vincent vividly articulated the vision: "Your convent will be the house of the sick; your cell, a hired room; your chapel, the parish church; your cloister, the streets of the city or the wards of the hospital."[10] Louise and Monseigneur Vincent worked together to meet the needs of the poor until their deaths a few months apart in 1660.

WHAT CAN WE LEARN?

I love to contemplate and to share the story of the generation of saints because their situation is so much like our own. Fifty

---

[9] Pierre Coste, *Monsieur Vincent: Le grand saint du grand siècle* (Paris: Desclée, de Brouwer et Cie, 1932), pp. 1, 290-291.

[10] *Butler's Lives of the Saints, Concise Edition*, Paul Burns, editor (Collegeville, MN: Liturgical Press, 2003), p. 119.

years after a council, after living through decades of intra-ecclesial chaos, conflict, and institutional decline, twenty-first-century Western Catholics are at a major turning point. What can we learn from this remarkable group of disciple-friends?

- *They were intentional disciples together.* Each member of the generation of saints was already personally seeking to follow Jesus as a disciple in the midst of his Church. But they also knew that we weren't meant to follow Jesus alone but as part of a community of disciples.

- *They were in mission together.* Clergy, religious, and laity; men and women from all classes and educational levels; Catholics with very different charisms, backgrounds, and vocations — all knew that they were collaborating in a great common mission. Lay men and women were taken seriously by clergy and religious as full partners — with a different office. They also regarded parishes as centers of missionary formation and outreach and as critical partners in mission with religious communities and other Catholic institutions.

- *They collaborated on a grand scale.* They readily and openly learned from one another and were influenced by one another. They assiduously mentored, encouraged, supported, and prayed for one another.

- *They were present and future oriented.* They looked to the historic riches of the Catholic faith for inspiration and guidance and then creatively applied the Tradition to the unique needs of *their* generation for the sake of future generations.

- *Apostolic creativity was the new normal.* The often-grim situations they faced were the catalyst of many new evangelically oriented communities, structures, outreaches, devotions, and spiritual resources.

- *They expected God to act.* They took the supernatural seriously and expected that the Holy Spirit would guide and inspire them, so they knew that ongoing discernment was critical. They also expected God to do things through them and provide for them in ways that were truly extraordinary.

- *They were deeply prayerful.* They knew that all spiritual and cultural transformation begins and ends with individuals encountering God in a profound way. They were especially aware of the incredible importance of corporate intercessory prayer to lay the foundation for fruitful evangelization.

- *They were faithful unto death.* They knew that significant change was the fruit of a long obedience in the same direction and were prepared to devote their entire lives to answering God's call.

Are we open to, are we willing to answer God's call with the same passion and lifelong obedience that enabled the generation of saints to transform French Catholicism and impact their entire nation for seven generations? Are we willing to answer the call and pay the price necessary to become a new generation of saints, through which God can do extraordinary things in our time? St. Vincent de Paul said it best:

So, our vocation is to go, not just to one parish, not just to one diocese, but all over the world; and to do what? To set people's hearts on fire, to do what the Son of

God did. He came to set the world on fire in order to inflame it with His love. What do we have to desire but that it may burn and consume everything.... It's true, then, that I'm sent not only to love God but to make Him loved. It's not enough for me to love God, if my neighbor doesn't love Him.[11]

———

SHERRY ANNE WEDDELL is the author of *Forming Intentional Disciples: The Path to Knowing and Following Jesus*. She co-founded and serves as Co-Director of the Catherine of Siena Institute, an affiliated international ministry of the Western Dominican Province. In 1993, she created the first charism-discernment process specifically designed for Catholics and has developed numerous unique formation resources that are used around the world.

---

[11] St. Vincent de Paul, *Vincentian Encyclopedia*, "Homily of Cardinal Rodé: On the occasion of the 350th anniversary of the death of Saint Vincent de Paul and Saint Louise de Marillac" (Rome, September 25, 2010), http://famvin .org/wiki/Homily_of_Cardinal_Rod%C3%A9.

CHAPTER TWO

Praying It Forward: Intercession and the Transformation of Your Parish

Keith Strohm

"You want us to do *what?*" Karen asked, shock sending her voice nearly an octave higher than normal.

I worked hard to keep the smile from showing on my face. It's not that I delight in torturing others, but I have to admit I enjoy moving people outside their comfort zones. And the fifteen parishioners sitting around me were definitely outside their zone of comfort.

"We're going to go out in pairs," I replied, "and each pair will head to a different street around the parish church. Once there, we'll walk the street and stop in front of each home to pray for the people who live in that house."

The gathered parishioners began muttering now, and the discontented sound grew louder. Clearly, this wasn't going to be as easy as I'd hoped.

ROAD TO RENEWAL

Nearly two years earlier, the deaths of our parish's retired pastor and our then-current pastor (only two days apart) rocked our community. When the new pastor, Father Ed Pelrine, settled in, he found a parish that was in need of renewal but filled with wonderful people. Like many parishes in the United States, a small group of parishioners were doing most of the work (financially and physically) to keep the ministries, apostolates, and life of the parish going. The physical side of our campus, which had been largely left alone over the years, needed some serious attention. To top it off, we had a strong Catholic school but little participation by school parents in the life of the parish. This was a parish firmly rooted in maintenance mode.

Father Ed understood that the "secret" to renewal for our parish wouldn't be found in a single program but rather a concerted effort at evangelization and the building of a culture of discipleship. To that end, he brought me on as the Director of Faith Formation a year after he came to the parish and asked me to focus on evangelization and the making of disciples. Together, we specifically worked on restructuring and renewing the RCIA program and youth ministry, and in general began the process of evangelizing the wider community. We knew we would have to spend time "preparing the soil" in order for the message of renewal through Christ to spread. We were not prepared for how rocky that soil would be.

In the book *Forming Intentional Disciples*, Sherry Weddell identifies a "culture of silence" that exists within Catholic parishes. This culture works against the spread of the Gospel by reinforcing attitudes that make it difficult for people to speak about their relationship with Jesus to others. Therefore, discipleship and personal relationship with Christ seem abnormal, "Protestant" or, worse, are not even dreamed of as possible.

At our parish, all of the detrimental effects of the culture of silence were in full force. Outside of a small percentage of parishioners who were intentional disciples of Jesus Christ, a transformative, life-giving personal relationship with Jesus was not on the radar for most members of our community. These were wonderful, giving, and friendly people who just did not know that they did not know. We experienced a great deal of passive resistance during this time.

In addition to the power of the culture of silence, we quickly found ourselves contending with the enemy. The apostle Paul clearly spells out the reality of the spiritual dimensions of battle in his letter to the Ephesians:

> For we are not contending against flesh and blood, but against the principalities, against the powers, against the world rulers of this present darkness, against the spiritual hosts of wickedness in the heavenly places. (Ephesians 6:12, RSV)

In his desire to renew and transform our parish along the trajectory of discipleship, Father Ed was pushing back against the kingdom that opposes the Kingdom of God. And the enemy responded. Both Father Ed and I experienced this in several ways, but the most frustrating was a kind of "wall" that seemed to rise up every time he preached or I taught. In conversation, we were both surprised that we described our experiences in such similar ways: we could both "feel" our words slamming into a barrier before they reached the gathered people. We were even more surprised when this same experience was mentioned by other guest speakers we brought into our community.

I have been a teacher with the Catherine of Siena Institute for many years, and I've taught the Institute's workshop on spiritual gifts discernment too many times to count. I've seen the power and fruitfulness of charisms in my own work and in the life of the parishes I've visited. God has gifted his people with spiritual gifts for the sake of our mission. Therefore, even though this was a period of great frustration, I knew that we had to gather together the community and begin to intercede for our parish if we wanted to start bearing fruit. Even more, I knew we had to identify gifted intercessors to break through the cultural and spiritual obstacles around us in a timely fashion.

THE POWER OF INTERCESSION

When I give retreats or talks, I often describe intercessory prayer as God's "Shock and Awe Campaign," because the fruit of individual and corporate intercession is often an overwhelming display of God's mercy, providence, and deliverance that changes the spiritual climate around a person or a place and transforms situations. Intercessory prayer disrupts the "infrastructure" of the enemy, by which I mean it weakens and destroys the network of lies, fear, intimidation, and confusion — the tools and strategies used by Satan to keep persons and situations away from God's peace, clarity, and redeeming love. In changing the spiritual climate around a person or community, this kind of prayer helps till the soil of the heart and prepares it to receive the seed of the Gospel.

Intercessory prayer is, however, more than simply coming before God with our prayers of supplication. When we engage in intercession, we participate in a sustained and intimate pleading before the Lord for someone else. Sister Ann Shields, in her book *Intercession: A Guide to Effective Prayer*, writes that "as intercessors, we literally 'go between' the Lord and those we are praying for, asking him to show them his mercy and blessing."[1] Some intercessors refer to this as "standing in the

---

[1]   Sister Ann Shields, S.G.L., *Intercession: A Guide to Effective Prayer* (Cincinnati: St. Anthony Messenger Press, 2004), p. 29.

gap" for someone else. They base this phrase on the passage from Ezekiel where the Lord is chastising the nation of Israel, and he speaks to the prophet saying: "Thus I have searched among them for someone who would build a wall or stand in the breach before me to keep me from destroying the land; but I found no one" (Ezekiel 22:30).

Intercessory prayer is woven deeply into the "spiritual DNA" of Catholics. Scripture is filled with people who stood in the gap for others — Abraham interceded with God on behalf of Sodom (Genesis 18), Moses offered to take God's wrath upon himself so that the Israelites could be spared (Exodus 32), Aaron made atonement for the Israelites (Numbers 17), and Samuel offered sacrifices so that the Israelites would triumph over the Philistines (1 Samuel 7). All of these examples of intercession were foreshadows of the coming intercession of the Son of God, who fulfilled all the promises God made in the Old Testament and who now "is always able to save those who approach God through him, since he lives forever to make intercession for them" (Hebrews 7:25).

Jesus Christ is the perfect intercessor, who pleads for us at the right hand of God. Rather than making our own attempts at intercession unnecessary, it is the person of Jesus who makes our intercession possible. We who were baptized into his death so that we might share in the life of the Risen Christ (Romans 6:3-4) also now live out the various dimensions of that life.

In other words, what Christ does now in eternity, we are called to do now in the world because of our baptism. Out of his great love for us, Jesus allows us to participate in his ministry of intercession, and he gives all of us his Spirit to strengthen our prayer and make it fruitful and effective (Romans 8:26). In addition, the Lord calls and gifts particular individuals with a charism for intercession that empowers their prayer for others.

Paul highlights the fundamental nature of intercession in the life of Christians in his first letter to Timothy:

First of all, then, I ask that supplications, prayers, petitions, and thanksgivings be offered for everyone, for kings and for all in authority, that we may lead a quiet and tranquil life in all devotion and dignity. (1 Timothy 2:1-2)

Intercession is so essential to the life of a disciple that the Church includes it in every celebration of the Holy Sacrifice of the Mass — as we implore the Lord to hear our prayers on behalf of the Church, the world, and our local community. The history of the Church is also filled with men and women — many of them saints — who persevered in intercession for others. Perhaps one of the most well known, and beloved, of these saints is Thérèse of Lisieux. Such was the fruitfulness and intensity of her intercessory prayer that she holds the title co-patron of the missions, despite having never sallied forth to do missionary work and, instead, living much of her short life within a cloister.

If we focus on the power of intercessory prayer, however, we inevitably come face to face with a dilemma: History (the world's and our own) is filled with "unanswered" prayers — or at least prayers which have not been answered the way that we hoped they would. People's hearts are still turned against God, our family members still fall ill and, sometimes, never recover despite our most fervent prayers. Intercessory prayer rests at the confluence of the mystery of God's mercy and the mystery of suffering. In reality, intercessory prayer is not a magic formula or a silver bullet; it's not a kind of extended arm on a divine slot machine that we only need to pull in order to line up three cherries and hit the miracle jackpot.

Prayer does not change God. Theologians have been teaching that for almost 2,000 years. He is immutable, unchangeable. If our prayers were to somehow change God, then we would have to admit that there was something deficient within God and he would, by definition, cease to be God. On the other hand, if God is, indeed, unchangeable, then aren't intercessory prayers really a waste of time?

This truly is quite a dilemma.

Our way through it, though, lies in an exploration of the nature of God and an understanding of causality — for which the thought of Thomas Aquinas, a medieval Dominican philosopher, will come in quite handy. Wait! Don't fall asleep yet! I promise you this will be quick, painless, and potentially enlightening.

For Thomas (as for many Christian philosophers), God was the primary cause of all creation — the source of existence. God created all living creatures and set them within the boundaries of his creation. Rather than simply setting everything in motion and then withdrawing to observe from a distance like some divine watchmaker, God chose to work through his creation "from the abundance of his goodness, imparting to creatures also the dignity of causing."[2] We, therefore, are the secondary causes through whom God works to fulfill his plan.

In this sense, our prayers of intercession are "always already" a response to what God is doing. When we are moved to pray for others, we are cooperating with God's will. Rachel Erdman, a theologian, summarizes this beautifully:

> I think the problem people have understanding prayer is that we tend to think of God as "responding" to our requests, when in reality it is only through the work of

---

2 Brian Davies, *The Thought of Thomas Aquinas* (Oxford: Clarendon Press, 1992), p. 163.

God the Holy Spirit that we are able to pray in the first place. It is God, always active in creation, who initiates the prayer in us — it is we who respond.[3]

Intercessory prayer, then, is initiated by the Holy Spirit so that we might dispose ourselves to the divine will and earnestly pray for its manifestation here on earth. In this, Jesus' instruction to his disciples regarding prayer is to be our model. The Lord's Prayer petitions the Father so that his will might be done "on earth as it is in heaven" (Matthew 6:10, RSV).

Pope Francis acknowledges this reality when he speaks about intercessory prayer in his apostolic exhortation *The Joy of the Gospel* (*Evangelii Gaudium*):

> The great men and women of God were great intercessors. Intercession is like a "leaven" in the heart of the Trinity. It is a way of penetrating the Father's heart and discovering new dimensions which can shed light on concrete situations and change them. We can say that God's heart is touched by our intercession, yet in reality he is always there first. What our intercession achieves is that his power, his love and his faithfulness are shown ever more clearly in the midst of the people. (283)

Seen this way, fruitfulness and effectiveness in prayer do not rely on personal effort or reciting the right words, but in "penetrating the Father's heart," aligning our will and desire with the divine and perfect will of our heavenly Father. This understanding sheds light on Jesus' own words that "whatever you ask in my name, I will do" (John 14:13).

---

[3]   Rachel Erdman, "Bending the King's Ear," *Australian eJournal of Theology* 20.1 (April 2013), p. 56.

To ask something in Jesus' name does not mean to throw out a prayer of petition and then tack on the name of Jesus as if it activated the power of the prayer like a magic word or formula. To pray in Jesus' name is to ask for what Jesus would ask for — not in an abstract "What would Jesus do?" kind of way, but actively to seek and ask him what he desires and then to listen with an open heart for the response. This is a pattern that I see repeated again and again in the life of mature intercessors — they do not so much come to God with their list of needs, but rather dispose themselves to the Holy Spirit so that he leads them in what they should pray for.

When we have raised up generations of such men and women at the parish level, we will truly begin to see the fruit of sustained corporate intercession in our evangelization and formation efforts. The question is: How do we raise up that generation?

Calling All Prayer Warriors

After reaching the conclusion about gathering intercessors to pray for the community during my first year on staff, I was stuck wrestling with that very question. I knew that I especially wanted to foster a cadre of gifted intercessors, but our staff — let alone the wider parish — did not yet have a common language around charisms and their discernment. I was also reluctant to post something in the bulletin that would appeal to gifted intercessors. I think many parish bulletins are too filled up with language and shorthand (like RCIA, CHRP, and so forth) that appeal to a small subsection of parish "insiders" but remain largely incomprehensible to those who might be in earlier thresholds of their spiritual journey.

Having taught the *Called & Gifted* workshop for many years, I did know that those with a charism of intercessory prayer share some characteristics in common. First off, they experience praying for others as one of the most powerful ways that God works in the world, and they have a particular passion for standing in the gap. It isn't unusual for a gifted intercessor to be in prayer for hours and then emerge refreshed and energized, for example. In addition, these men and women often wake up in the middle of the night with a particular person, situation, or geographic place for which they feel led to pray. Many gifted intercessors feel as if their prayer is being directed by the Holy Spirit, almost as if he were "praying through" them, and they usually have a sense when they are "done." Most importantly, those with a charism of intercessory prayer see remarkable, often miraculous, fruit from their prayer for others.

When the time was right, I wrote a very general article for our bulletin advertising an upcoming "Evening of Intercession." In the article, I gave a very quick definition of intercessory prayer, and I invited anyone who might be interested to come — even if they had never heard about intercessory prayer and knew nothing about it. Imagine my surprise when almost fifty parishioners showed up! I asked for a show of hands from those people who understood what intercessory prayer was. Only a few shot up. Clearly, I couldn't move right into an evening of spontaneous praise, worship, and intercession. I had to lay some groundwork ... and fast!

We opened with a brief prayer and Scripture reflection, and then I gave more background on intercessory prayer. After that foundation, I knew that my would-be intercessors needed some safe, non-threatening experiences of intercession. I had consulted with a friend and colleague earlier and had already settled on using the Chaplet of Divine Mercy as a starting point. I broke the gathering up into five groups (one for each decade of the chaplet), and I asked each group to identify areas within our parish community where God's Spirit already seemed to be at work.

After about fifteen minutes, I called them all together, and each group read off the areas that they had identified. I then informed them that each group should pick an announcer. We would go through the Chaplet of Divine Mercy, and at the start of each decade of the chaplet, the announcer from one of the groups would list the areas their group identified. We would then offer that decade for the intensification of the action of the Holy Spirit in those areas.

Feedback from that meeting was exceptionally positive. We met again the following month. This time, I had each group list the obstacles they felt kept men and women in our local civic community from hearing and responding to the Gospel message. Each group led a decade of the Divine Mercy Chaplet, praying that God would remove those specific obstacles. Again, the participants were happy and excited to pray in this way.

We continued to meet monthly. Fewer and fewer people showed up, but the ones who did seemed to be energized by our intercessory sessions. Without a lot of direction from me, those with the charisms of intercessory prayer eventually became the majority in that group. We gradually shifted from more standard, rote prayers and began to experiment with Scripture reading, silence, and then spontaneous intercession. This continued for several more months until the fateful evening when I decided to send them out in twos to go prayer walking. I knew that we eventually wanted to send out "missionaries" from our parish into our local community, and I wanted to make sure that we had gifted individuals (and the general parish community) comfortable with "covering" the entire village in prayer before our evangelists went out.

There was a little more hemming and hawing, but I managed, through the grace of God, to cajole them out. We all grabbed our partner, said a quick prayer, and then walked and prayed through our assigned route. When everyone returned to the parish church, I could sense a buzz in the air, a kind of energy that I hadn't really seen among many of our parishioners. Of course, they were excited that they conquered their fears and did something they might never have done without a little push. But there was something else. In talking to a few of these intercessors later that evening, it was clear they had experienced, briefly, a greater sense of participating in the redemptive work of Christ — a kind of intimacy in the "work" of prayer that they had never felt before.

As amazing as it was to see this group of mostly neophyte intercessors change and begin to transform into bold prayer warriors, the effect of their prayers on our parish was even more powerful. In the sixth months since their first meeting, the wall that Father Ed and I experienced between ourselves and the parishioners disappeared. People began to respond in even greater numbers and depth to the Gospel message, as they heard it preached at Mass, during the RCIA, and during our four-week homegrown evangelization process. The sense of disunity and opposition that seemingly surrounded our staff broke apart. Staff relationships and interaction became healthier. New staff members joined us, and disciples from other parts of the archdiocese began to show up at our doorstep. In short, the spiritual climate of our parish has changed — and that has had a positive impact on every other area of our mission.

Four years after we began this process of intercession, we are finding an even greater need for it. We have begun sending out a small team of missionaries to start evangelizing the local community. The Lord has also led us to begin a small healing ministry, which is growing at a regular pace, and our process for helping baptized Christians and the unbaptized become disciples of Christ in the midst of his Church is growing beyond the infrastructure we currently have.

We are still very much a parish in transition. We are not spiritual giants. So far, no one here has had to tie himself to a pew to stop floating in the air during Mass (a la St. Joseph of Cupertino), and we do not have any Marian locutionists among us. We bicker, gossip, squabble, celebrate, and support one another like normal people. We are ordinary men and women whom God has equipped to do extraordinary things for his Kingdom — and we have helped to unleash that divine empowerment through sustained intercession.

Because of that, the number of intentional disciples in our parish has doubled in five years. We are no longer focused on maintenance. Our hearts and minds are gradually opening up to mission. The Lord continues to move us further and further out of our comfort zones as a community, and I find myself sending up a quick prayer of gratitude every time I hear one of our parishioners cry out, "You want us to do *what*?"

Because God is about to move.

KEITH STROHM is the Director of Evangelization & Faith Formation for Queen of the Rosary Parish in the northwestern suburbs of Chicago and a third-year candidate for the diaconate in the Archdiocese of Chicago. He is also a longtime teacher and collaborator with the Catherine of Siena Institute. In his copious free time, he gathers his thoughts, reflections, and ideas regarding evangelization and ministry at www.ablaze -ministries.org. Keith lives in the suburbs of Chicago with his wife, Debbie, daughter, Siena, and two goofy Siberian huskies.

CHAPTER THREE

Co-Responsible for the Mission of Christ

Father Michael Fones, O.P.

For many Catholics in the United States, taking the faith seriously means getting involved in the local parish. It might be going to a weekday Mass, joining a Bible study, exploring a men's or women's group, or going on a retreat. And, too often, those of us involved in parochial ministry — or any Church ministry, for that matter — can unwittingly promote that instinct. We who are pastoral leaders need laypeople to help with our many programs and ministries! In most parishes, at least among those that have not made a concerted effort to evangelize, there is a greater demand for help with various ministries and outreach programs than there is a supply. But too often, that is as far as our imagination takes us.

And yet, the charisms given to the baptized, while ordered toward the building up of the Church,[1] are not simply given for specific Church ministries. For the laity, especially, the charisms are given for the apostolate — God's ongoing mission to the

---

[1] "Whether extraordinary or simple and humble, charisms are graces of the Holy Spirit which directly or indirectly benefit the Church, ordered as they are to her building up, to the good of men, and to the needs of the world" (*Catechism of the Catholic Church* [CCC], 799).

world. Father Yves Congar, the great Dominican theologian whose reflections on the laity were to become so important to the bishops at the Second Vatican Council, observed:

> History shows that the apostolate of the laity is only taken seriously when a real "world" exists to confront the Church, and the Church is aware of it. Then the tension is felt for what it is, a tension between the Church, seed and sacrament of the kingdom of God, and the world. In those conditions priests and laity feel themselves to be called and yoked to the same task: the laity are no longer mere passengers in a ship navigated by the clergy alone: they are, in their own place, part of the ship's company.[2]

Being "yoked" together for the same call and tasks implies that the clergy and laity are co-responsible for both. So let's explore what that means and examine a built-in structure for that co-responsibility.

Co-Responsibility for the Church's Mission

If your parish has a mission statement, have you read it? Does it have any reference to the world beyond the parish parking lot? If you have read it, have you committed it to memory? A mission statement should direct the efforts of a community, and all newly proposed and ongoing endeavors ought to be evaluated in light of it. The Church was given a mission by the resurrected Lord shortly before his ascension:

---

2   Yves Congar, O.P., *Christians Active in the World* (New York: Herder & Herder, 1968), p. 8.

"[1] Go … [2] make disciples of all nations, [3] baptizing them in the name of the Father, and of the Son, and of the holy Spirit, [4] teaching them to observe all that I have commanded you." (Matthew 28:19-20)

This simple four-point mission makes it clear that the building up of the Church mentioned in paragraph 799 of the *Catechism* is not limited to the addition of programs, ministries, or projects in the local parish. In fact, primarily it involves the spread of the Gospel and the inclusion into the Body of Christ of all the peoples of the world, along with working for the good of each individual and responding to secular needs.

Pope Francis has urged us to have the audacity and courage to "step outside" ourselves and "go to those who do not attend Mass, to those who have quit or are indifferent."[3] It *does* take great courage for a Catholic — whether ordained, religious, or lay — to venture outside the relatively safe confines of the parish physical plant. Our society is increasingly secular and more intolerant of truth claims. One characteristic of a secular society is that it is more hospitable to those who do *not* profess a faith than to those who *do*.

When Pope St. John XXIII convened the Second Vatican Council, he intended that the bishops address the widening chasm between the Church and the secular world, and the gap between the religious and civic lives of individual Catholics. With prophetic clarity, he saw a modern society that was "characterized by great material progress but without a corresponding advance in the moral sphere. Thence a weakening in aspirations towards the values of the spirit; thence the tendency to seek only the earthly pleasures that technological

3 "A Big Heart Open to God," an interview with Pope Francis, by Antonio Spadaro, S.J., in *America* magazine (September 30, 2013), http://www.americamagazine.org/pope-interview.

progress brings so easily within the reach of all; thence also a quite new and disturbing fact: the existence of a militant atheism operating all over the world."[4]

If this world is to hear the Gospel, the bishops realized, the laity, who are active participants in both the Church and secular society, must be co-responsible with the hierarchy for the Church's mission of evangelization. In a clear re-affirmation of Jesus' great commission, the bishops of the council proclaimed, "The apostolate of the Church *and of all its members* is primarily designed to manifest Christ's message by words and deeds and to communicate His grace to the world."[5]

And this is no new invention of a Church short on priests. In the Gospel of John, when the Risen Jesus appears to his disciples, he gives the Holy Spirit to them through his own life-giving breath, and from that moment, the mission of Christ becomes the mission of the whole Church, his Body, animated by the Spirit.[6] The council fathers were adamant, indeed, that "the laity derive the right and duty to the apostolate from their union with Christ the head" and by immersion into his life through baptism and confirmation "they are assigned to the apostolate by the Lord Himself."[7]

The co-responsibility of the laity with the hierarchy in bringing Christ to the world is carried out primarily through their secular endeavors: their work, family life, participation in civic groups, and participation in the political process. They are to "seek the kingdom of God by engaging in temporal affairs and by ordering them according to the plan of God"[8] and through

---

4   Pope John XXIII, *Humanae Salutis.*
5   Decree on the Apostolate of the Laity (*Apostolicam Actuositatem*), 6, emphasis added.
6   John 20:21; cf. Matthew 28:19; Luke 24:47-48; Acts 1:8.
7   Decree on the Apostolate of the Laity (*Apostolicam Actuositatem*), 3.
8   Dogmatic Constitution on the Church (*Lumen Gentium*), 31.

their sharing in the priesthood of Christ, "consecrate the world itself to God"[9] in the unfolding of their baptismal grace. This is the unique way they contribute to evangelization and fulfill their responsibility for the conversion of the structures and institutions of society.[10]

Clergy and religious, as baptized members of Christ's Body, also share in this responsibility to evangelize, but in ways different from each other and from the laity. Religious who profess poverty, chastity, and obedience are freed by the evangelical counsels to dedicate themselves to deepening the relationship with the poor, chaste, obedient Christ to which every disciple is called.

The ministerial priesthood is directed to and at the service of the common priesthood of the faithful (see CCC 1547). Sharing in Christ's work of building up and leading the Church, the clergy call members of the Body of Christ to conversion through the Word, to sanctity through the sacraments, and to unity in the Spirit for the sake of the mission.

One of the difficulties, I think, that occurred after the Second Vatican Council centered on a desire to enhance the status of the laity in the Church in a way that neglected the essential difference between the common and ministerial priesthood. This occurred because, as Father Congar would have predicted, in parishes where the apostolate of the laity in the world was ignored, the only way imagined to "enhance" the dignity of the laity was to get them more involved in the ministries of the parish and to encroach upon the offices and duties of the pastor.

And why was the apostolate of the laity in the world ignored? That answer, I believe, points to a fundamental and ongoing problem: How many members of the clergy and laity

---

[9] Ibid., 34.
[10] Ibid., 36.

have had the sort of encounter with the Risen Lord that Pope Emeritus Benedict XVI and Pope Francis have referred to on so many occasions?[11] We seem not to have experienced the Good News as *good*, and until that happens, the apostolate of the laity in the world — and the new evangelization itself — will be dead in the water.

Pope Francis gets to the essence of evangelization in *The Joy of the Gospel* when he writes: "The primary reason for evangelizing is the love of Jesus which we have received, the experience of salvation which urges us to ever greater love of him. What kind of love would not feel the need to speak of the beloved, to point him out, to make him known?"[12]

The Decree on the Apostolate of the Laity (*Apostolicam Actuositatem*) envisioned laypeople involved in "certain functions which are more closely connected with pastoral duties, such as the teaching of Christian doctrine, certain liturgical actions, and the care of souls."[13] By entrusting these functions to members of the laity, a kind of "working with" was established, but it is a "working with" that is preceded by and dependent upon delegation, because immediately after allowing for this sharing of pastoral duties, the bishops noted, "by virtue of this mission, the laity are *fully subject to higher ecclesiastical control* in the performance of this work."[14] The person in authority delegates but retains full responsibility for the outcome.

---

[11] For example, Pope Benedict claimed in his homily at his Pallium Mass on April 24, 2005, "There is nothing more beautiful than to be surprised by the Gospel, by the encounter with Christ. There is nothing more beautiful than to know Him and to speak to others of our friendship with Him."

[12] Pope Francis, *The Joy of the Gospel* (*Evangelii Gaudium*), 264.

[13] Decree on the Apostolate of the Laity (*Apostolicam Actuositatem*), 24.

[14] Ibid., emphasis added.

OUTWARD AND APOSTOLIC

Just as the relationship between Christ and the Church is a nuptial mystery of mutual self-giving love (cf. Ephesians 5:25-32), so, too, the relationship between pastor and laity has a nuptial character that transcends the hierarchical. As the mutual love of husband and wife bears fruit in the begetting and raising of children (for which they are obviously co-responsible!), the clergy and laity *together* with God's grace are co-responsible for responding to the commission of Christ. And the fruitfulness of that co-responsibility is making disciples — spiritual children — of all the nations. So what might this co-responsibility look like in a parish?

In every parish, the pastor, according to canon law,[15] is responsible for a multitude of tasks:

1. Making the Eucharist the center of parish life and promoting other sacraments.

2. Instructing the laity in the faith and catechesis.

3. Knowing the faithful.

4. Cooperating with the bishop and other pastors.

5. *Fostering the works of the Gospel, including social justice.*

6. *Seeking out the poor, the afflicted, the lonely, and exiles.*

7. *Promoting marriage and family life.*

---

[15] Code of Canon Law (*Codex Iuris Canonici* [CIC]), 528-529.

8. *Fostering the role of the laity in the Church's mission.*

9. *Evangelizing with the help of the laity.*

As a former pastor, I know that this list is enough to make any cleric recognize his inadequacy for the office and the need to rely upon Christ and his grace. It also underscores that cooperation is required with other clerics, religious, and members of the laity. But as we examine this list, it seems that some of the tasks are clearly pastoral and oriented toward parish life, while others have a more apostolic and *secular* focus. The first four tasks will be areas in which the pastor can delegate responsibility to members of his staff and qualified laypeople. Tasks five through nine (aspects that are italicized) will be areas that can extend beyond the members of the parish, and thus be areas of fruitful co-responsibility with the laity.

Furthermore, because the family is the domestic Church,[16] parents have, so to speak, a "pastoral" responsibility to evangelize and catechize their children and promote the sacraments, so there are opportunities for genuine cooperation between pastors and the parents in their parish in these areas.

Still, the aspect of life in the Church where it is most clear that co-responsibility is not only possible but also necessary is the proclamation through words and actions of the Gospel of Jesus Christ to the world. Parish pastoral councils may suggest a model ideally suited to fostering this co-responsibility. Such a council, *if it had an exclusively apostolic focus*, could be an instrument by which the Holy Spirit works to unite a community in a common purpose.

---

[16] Dogmatic Constitution on the Church (*Lumen Gentium*), 11.

RE-IMAGINING PARISH PASTORAL COUNCILS

The presence of the Holy Spirit in the Church and her members today is an ongoing revelation of God's providence, healing, and redeeming power. The Holy Spirit helps dispose people to receive the gift of faith in Jesus Christ, which has the capacity to overthrow divisions humanity creates among its members. St. Paul gave witness to this power when he told the Galatians "there is neither Jew nor Greek, there is neither slave nor free person, there is not male and female; for you are all one in Christ Jesus" (Galatians 3:28; see also Colossians 3:11 and Romans 10:12).

Father Yves Congar, O.P., recognized that the activity of the Spirit in history allows us to interpret the events of history in light of the life, death, and resurrection of Jesus, so that reading the signs of the times as they are found in the secular realm is a theological activity of those who are living in his Spirit. Congar said:

> This means that the hierarchy is not enclosed within itself, that the movement of the Spirit is not like that of a one-way street. The Spirit is not monopolized by the "hierarchy" as though this were a kind of reservoir dispensing gifts from above.... All this signifies a reciprocity and exchange between the delegated office of Christ's institution and the personal life through the grace of the Holy Spirit.[17]

---

[17] Yves Congar, O.P., "Pneumatology Today," *The American Ecclesiastical Review* 167, no. 7 (1973), p. 446. I am indebted to Father Anthony Oelrich for this quote, which he referenced in his talk, "What Is It to Think with the Church?" given at the 2014 Convocation of Fellows of the Dominican School of Philosophy and Theology, Berkeley, CA, January 31, 2014.

The bishops gathered at the Second Vatican Council envisioned the clergy and laity working together in a way that connected the local Church to the world in which it is immersed. In the Decree on the Apostolate of the Laity, they wrote: "The laity should accustom themselves to working in the parish in union with their priests, bringing to the Church community their own and the world's problems as well as questions concerning human salvation, all of which they should examine and resolve by deliberating in common."[18]

Later, in the same decree, the bishops encouraged the establishment of councils on the parochial, interparochial, interdiocesan, and even international level,[19] which would

> assist the apostolic work of the Church either in the field of evangelization and sanctification or in the charitable, social, or other spheres, and here it is fitting that the clergy and Religious should cooperate with the laity. While preserving the proper character and autonomy of each organization, these councils will be able to promote the mutual coordination of various lay associations and enterprises.[20]

Notice that the bishops indicate that with regard to the evangelization and sanctification of the secular realm, the clergy and religious *cooperate with the laity*.

While the parish pastoral council has evolved since the council and, at its best, functions as a visioning body that helps the pastor with pastoral planning and the setting of pastoral

---

[18] Decree on the Apostolate of the Laity (*Apostolicam Actuositatem*), 10.

[19] The 1973 circular letter on councils, *Omnes Christifideles*, later discouraged councils on the inter-diocesan, provincial, regional, national, and international levels.

[20] Decree on the Apostolate of the Laity (*Apostolicam Actuositatem*), 26.

goals, such councils seldom turn their attention to the larger mission of the local Church, which is evangelization and the sanctification of the local secular environment. In other words, our parish pastoral councils tend to be focused inward, and perhaps that is in their very nature, given their model.

Pope Benedict, in an address that opened a pastoral convention of the Diocese of Rome, expressed a desire that something change in the parish:

> It is necessary to improve pastoral structures in such a way that the co-responsibility of all the members of the People of God in their entirety is gradually promoted, with respect for vocations and for the respective roles of the consecrated and of lay people. This demands a change in mindset, particularly concerning lay people. They must no longer be viewed as "collaborators" of the clergy but truly recognized as "co-responsible," for the Church's being and action, thereby fostering the consolidation of a mature and committed laity. This common awareness of being Church of all the baptized in no way diminishes the responsibility of parish priests. It is precisely your task, dear parish priests, to nurture the spiritual and apostolic growth of those who are already committed to working hard in the parishes. They form the core of the community that will act as a leaven for the others.[21]

One way a pastoral structure — namely, the parish pastoral council — could be improved to promote co-responsibility between the laity and clergy for the mission of the Church

---

[21] Pope Benedict XVI, Opening of the Pastoral Convention of the Diocese of Rome on the Theme: "Church Membership and Pastoral Co-Responsibility," May 26, 2009.

would be for the council to expand in scope — and, perhaps, in membership — with a mandate to help call the parish community to common apostolic initiatives, as well as to help the parish recognize and support the apostolic initiatives of individual members of the community.

Years ago, when I was director of the campus Catholic ministry at the University of Oregon in Eugene, I tried to call attention to the apostolic endeavors of some of the parishioners — for example, a periodontist who provided free dental care to the homeless on her days off and an attorney who offered *pro bono* legal aid. I was hoping that other members of the community would join with them.

My efforts failed, but several problems came to light in that failure. It seems that those wonderful laypeople did not recognize the work they were doing as truly ecclesial, rising from their participation in the Church's communion. Nor did I know that in an inchoate way I was attempting to exercise a bit of pastoral governance by supporting the pastoral initiatives of a few of the disciples in the flock. Finally, there was no structure or process to help identify and promote individual apostolic initiatives, nor a means to foster the formation of group initiatives.

The Decree on the Apostolate of the Laity identifies the individual apostolate, like that of those generous parishioners, as the origin of the whole lay apostolate.[22] Such generosity flows from a truly Christian life whose source is the ongoing encounter with the Risen Christ. What is more, all laypersons "are called to this type of apostolate and obliged to engage in it."[23] As we focus on evangelization in our parishes, we should expect more lay men and women responding to the Holy Spirit's invitation

---

[22] Decree on the Apostolate of the Laity (*Apostolicam Actuositatem*), 16.
[23] Ibid.

to apply their faith in the world. But often, they may desire help in discerning how to do that.

This is where a re-imagining of how a parish pastoral council functions is so necessary. Ideally, a parish pastoral council advises the pastor about pastoral matters through study, research, prayer, and reflection. It seems there is no reason why a parish council could not also pursue the vision of the Vatican Council fathers in the Decree on the Apostolate of the Laity (10 and 26).

The first section encourages the laity, who by virtue of their secular character, experience the ills of their community firsthand to bring these problems to their pastor for discussion in light of the Church's teaching. This is not to suggest that "Father knows best," and that he can provide all the answers. Rather, the council and pastor together, knowing the people of the parish, could gather members of the community who are affected by the problem to hear as many aspects and perspectives as possible. The members of the council and the pastor could draw upon the expertise of other members of the parish or even the broader Catholic community in order to understand the complex dynamics that lie behind a particular problem in the secular community.

After listening — a lot! — about the problem, the pastor could help provide — or at least know where to look for — Scripture passages and Church teaching that might illuminate the problem. Reflecting on this input from the Church's wisdom would inform and guide discussions of the pastor and council on the application of the teaching in the particular setting of *this* local Church. The goal would be to find not necessarily *one* solution but, perhaps, a multifaceted approach that would engage a variety of people with different charisms.

This is one way in which the pastor shares in the co-responsibility of the Church's mission to the world. It also reflects the ecclesial reality of the Church as both institutional and charismatic. The Holy Spirit is at work through the office of the pastor, who, because of his relation to the bishop by virtue of ordination, has responsibility for the "unity of faith and also for sustaining the dynamism of the universal apostolate."[24] At the same time, he must be careful not to quench the Spirit at work in the charisms of the faithful, while being sure to "test the spirits to see whether they belong to God" (1 John 4:1) — i.e., ensure that whatever course of action is proposed is compatible with Christian doctrine.

A PARISH LOOKS OUTWARD

Let me give an example of a parish that is attempting something like this.[25] Holy Apostles Parish in Colorado Springs, Colorado, has had the same pastor, Father Paul Wicker, for over thirty years. The parish has had a consistent mission statement for quite some time: "By our prayer and actions we lovingly invite all to come home to God through Christ." The parish, using the model "Apostles of Hope," calls "each parishioner to be involved as an agent of hope in our community." The pastor and his staff have defined an "Apostle of Hope" as an individual actively living out the parish mission statement. These individuals recognize their life as a vocation in Christ, and they know they are disciples of Jesus who are gifted by God for the work he intends for them and are thus called and sent by him to bring his love into the world. The universal call to holiness

---

[24] J. Francis Cardinal Stafford, "Institutional and Charismatic Aspects: Quasi Coessential to the Church's Constitution," *L'Osservatore Romano* (English edition), April 26, 2000, p. 6.

[25] I am indebted to Father Paul Wicker and Mr. Sam Gioia, the pastoral business manager at Holy Apostles Catholic Church, Colorado Springs, CO, for sharing their vision and pastoral process with me.

and discipleship is regularly preached, and the characteristics of "Apostles of Hope" are spoken about regularly.

In 2011, Father Paul and his staff decided that to help more parishioners recognize that they were being called and sent by Christ into their local neighborhoods, they needed to better understand to whom he was sending them.

In order to do this, the parish held a synod for all the parishioners, which was organized into two sessions, each lasting four to six hours, and separated in time by about a month. At the first gathering, the staff presented the demographic data gathered on the people living within the parish boundaries. At that meeting, the parishioners identified nine groups of people to whom they could reach out: the elderly, the poor, the disabled, the immigrants, the single parent families, the youth, the military personnel and their families, the fallen-away Catholics, and the unchurched.

At the next assembly, parishioners were asked to reflect on how Christ might be calling individual members of his Body to respond to the real situations facing their neighbors. Directions for future ministerial outreach were also explored as participants answered this question: "If I feel called to help someone, but the resources I need are outside of my capability, how can my parish or other community organizations help me?"

The parish is structured in a way similar to most, but Father Paul has introduced some significant paradigmatic changes. For example, the pastor and staff see their role as animating the lay faithful to achieve their mission. Parish ministries are being reformed to provide education and formation in discipleship. One significant difference, however, flows from the follow-up to the synodal process.

After identifying nine focus groups of people within their parish boundaries, parishioners were invited to select one group that they felt called to reach out to in some way. These would be people whom the parishioner would interact with in the course of their daily life — at work, at home, or in the community. Since they routinely see or work with people in that focus group, they are best suited to both present the "Face of Christ" to those people as well as name the darkness which confronts them. Parishioners make a commitment publicly, simply by placing a small felt chalice on one of nine banners that line the perimeter of the church nave.

For each focus area, a commission of those interested in serving them was formed to coordinate an exploration of the specific needs of the people within the parish boundaries who belonged to that group. Those commissions then report to a twelve-member parish council, called the Governance Body, to emphasize that the orientation of their vision is outward, toward the men, women, and institutions that are found within their parish boundaries.

The Governance Body meets each month with the pastor and is composed of gifted laypeople identified as "Apostles of Hope" and appointed by the pastor as consultors with him because of their ability to plan for the future. As leaders of significant ministries in the parish, they have received a formation in the Church's teaching on the mission of the Church and the complementary roles of the clergy and laity in that mission. They are accountable to the pastor and know their role is to assist him in his governance of the gifts and common mission of the parish.

The pastor, with his Governance Body, coordinates the parish's outreach to the people in the focus groups. Using the Fritz model for creative processes,[26] they clearly describe the current reality they face and the desired result before identifying

---

[26] Robert Fritz, *The Path of Least Resistance: Learning to Become the Creative Force in Your Own Life* (New York: Random House, 1989).

action steps to transform the former into the latter.[27] The role of the staff is primarily to receive input and feedback from the pastor and his Governance Body and help coordinate the seventy ministries that are engaged in implementing the action steps, again, focusing on animating the lay faithful in group apostolates.

Three major resources help parishioners engage in their part of the mission given the whole Church by Christ: *ministries*, which are supervised by the Ministerial Staff; *focus groups*, which are called together by the Governance Body to provide insight into the groups of people living within the parish boundaries; and the *Apostles of Hope Coordination Team*, which connects individual "Apostles of Hope" with people in need.

DIFFICULTIES THAT STILL MUST BE OVERCOME

The parish still has a long way to go. According to Sam Gioia, the pastoral business manager and Father Paul's close collaborator, "One of the fundamental challenges in implementing the Apostles of Hope model is shifting ministries from *doing the work* of Christ to *animating the work* of Christ to be done by his disciples. For example, rather than measuring the impact of the social ministry by how many families they have helped, we are now asking, 'How many people are helping reach those families?' This is a fundamental shift. If we had five people in the social ministry, but were impacting 300 families, the challenge in

---

[27] A process of theological reflection could also be taught to and utilized by a parish council and pastor. One model, championed by James and Evelyn Whitehead (*Method in Ministry* [Lanham, MD: Sheed and Ward, 1995]) would bring parishioners' experiences, the Church's Scripture and Tradition, and an awareness of cultural attitudes and insights from social sciences into critical dialogue with one another in a three-step method of *attending, asserting*, and *pastoral response.*

the past would have been, 'How do we help 400 families?' The question today is 'Why are there only five of us doing this?'"

In addition, because people with particular charisms see very clearly particular needs and particular responses, sometimes the meetings of the Governance Body are fractious! Pope Francis anticipates this in his apostolic exhortation, *The Joy of the Gospel*. Yet he also reminds us of the hope we have because of the presence of the Holy Spirit, who waits for us to seek out his guidance:

> Differences between persons and communities can sometimes prove uncomfortable, but the Holy Spirit, who is the source of that diversity, can bring forth something good from all things and turn it into an attractive means of evangelization. Diversity must always be reconciled by the help of the Holy Spirit; he alone can raise up diversity, plurality and multiplicity while at the same time bringing about unity.[28]

Finally, one area that is not addressed in the model used at Holy Apostles has to do with individuals like the periodontist and the lawyer I mentioned earlier. Not every layperson must necessarily engage in the apostolate by participating in a group apostolate through their local parish.

> Indeed, the lay apostolate admits of different types of relationships with the hierarchy in accordance with the various forms and objects of this apostolate. For in the Church there are many apostolic undertakings which are established by the free choice of the laity and regulated by their prudent judgment. The mission of the Church

---

[28] Pope Francis, *The Joy of the Gospel* (*Evangelii Gaudium*), 117.

can be better accomplished in certain circumstances by undertakings of this kind, and therefore they are frequently praised or recommended by the hierarchy.[29]

One of the challenges many pastors and their staffs face involves identifying those anonymous disciples of Jesus Christ in our parishes who are attempting to apply their faith in their work, and through corporal and spiritual works of mercy in the secular realm. Undoubtedly, they could benefit tremendously from the support and encouragement of other parishioners and their pastor, yet they do not need to have their apostolate assimilated Borg-like into the parish ministerial program.

A CLOSING THOUGHT

In the Christian faith, there is only one sacrifice and only one priest: Jesus Christ. Every baptized member of his Body participates in that one priesthood and forms "a kingdom of priests" (Exodus 19:6; cf. Revelation 5:10) that shares in his prophetic and royal mission. The ordained exercise their share in this one priesthood as they stand in the person of Christ, the head of the Body, who came "not to be served but to serve" (Matthew 20:28, RSV) so as to help all the members of the Body grow in holiness, themselves included! The participation of the laity in the one priesthood of Christ is primarily directed toward the secular world, which they are to consecrate through every aspect of their lives. This world, which God so loves, is served by the laity when they denounce the evil they witness firsthand, nurture the good they find there, and "restore to creation all its original value."[30]

---

[29] Decree on the Apostolate of the Laity (*Apostolicam Actuositatem*), 24.
[30] Pope John Paul II, *Christifideles Laici*, 14.

None of this happens without the ongoing activity of the Spirit of truth, who arouses and sustains the discernment of clergy and laity as they work together to apply the faith to the real problems that confront the communities in which our local parishes and their members are embedded. And the desire and ability to respond to the brokenness endemic in society itself are products of the encounter with Jesus in the Spirit, through which we experience the mercy of God. From that encounter, and nurtured by sacramental graces, we begin the journey toward holiness.

As Pope Francis reminds us, "sanctity does not consist especially in doing extraordinary things, but in allowing God to act. It is the meeting of our weakness and the strength of his grace" and doing everything "with joy and humility, for the glory of God and as a service to our neighbor."[31]

The language of "co-responsibility" for the Church's mission works on two levels. First of all, Christ, our Divine Spouse, shares his mission with us, his Bride, and in no way are we sent by him to work in the world alone. "I am with you always," he says (Matthew 28:20). The Great Commission (Matthew 28:19) to "Go, therefore, and make disciples of all nations" has always been a joint venture between God and humanity, animated by the Spirit of mutual love the Son shares with the Father.

On the human level, the clergy and laity are co-responsible for the response to this commission, each with different, though complementary areas of emphasis — similar, in a way, to the equal, yet complementary roles of a husband and wife in a marriage. Rivalry or envy, self-inflation or belittling, will undermine our ability to work together and with Christ. Co-responsibility flourishes in a relationship marked by mutual respect, equal dignity, trust, and mutual affection.

---

[31] Pope Francis, General Audience, October 2, 2013.

Rev. Mr. James Keating expressed a consequence of the nuptial relationship between a pastor and parishioners in a reflection on priestly spirituality that captures my own experience as a pastor:

> As a spouse contemplates the spiritual and moral growth of his or her beloved since marriage, finding there a place to invest the meaning and purpose of nuptial self-giving, so the priest looks to the converted lives of the laity, and even deeper to the effects these lives have had upon the transformation of culture, to invest his life's purpose.[32]

I believe this is preeminently true of Jesus Christ, who invested his life — even to death — for us, his Bride, the Church, that we might be converted, holy and without blemish. Now, let us work in the world with him who is making all things new.[33]

———

FATHER MICHAEL FONES, O.P., entered the Order of Friars Preachers (Dominicans) in 1984, was ordained in 1992, and worked in campus ministry for twelve years before becoming the Co-Director of the Catherine of Siena Institute. In 2011, he was appointed to formation work for his province. He also teaches field education at the Dominican School of Philosophy and Theology in Berkeley, California.

---

[32] Rev. Mr. James Keating, "Priestly Spirituality, Seminary Formation, and Lay Mission," *Seminary Journal* 13:2 (2007), p. 86.

[33] Cf. Revelation 21:5.

CHAPTER FOUR

Intentional Disciples:
Bearing Spiritual Fruit
That Sustains

Bobby Vidal

Several years ago I found myself in the presence of an extraordinary lay apostle — a woman who was on the verge of discovering her personal vocation and where she was being "sent" to carry the light of the Gospel. As I listened to her story of how God was using her to reach others, I was struck by the magnitude of creative energy and profound boldness that flowed through her so naturally. Every week she arranged to meet with two female friends. They prayed, asking God to use them to touch the lives of the people they were about to meet, and then this woman led the others to a nearby neighborhood that was overcome with prostitution.

After determining it was safe to do so, she would go and knock on a motel-room door. It wasn't always the case that someone came readily to the door, but when the door finally opened she would introduce herself and ask the woman who stood before her if she wanted to pray. Surprisingly, only rarely did she meet with a negative response. Then, as she prayed, something astonishing would happen. The woman she was praying for would begin to find herself clothed with an overpowering sense of love and mercy. As this lay apostle continued to pray and then talk about Jesus, layer upon layer of trauma, anger, fear, and shame would begin to melt away.

This weekly apostolate was producing remarkable spiritual fruit. A large number of women who were stuck in a life of prostitution soon found hope and a restored sense of their dignity as children of God. God was doing something remarkable.

As I listened to her story, however, it became shockingly clear that the work of God in this woman was encountering remarkable obstacles. Equally shocking — those obstacles were coming from her parish community, which failed to support and understand her work.

As more and more women who were trapped in the life of prostitution encountered the love of God, new challenges emerged in her apostolate that were too complex and demanding for her to deal with on her own. Not knowing where to turn for help, she sought the aid of her parish — but no one was willing to help her. Not only were her fellow parishioners unwilling to help, but no one could assist her in discerning what God was calling her to do next.

She felt certain that God had called her to this work, but she began to ask herself: Was she called merely to pray with these women and talk to them about Jesus, or was God calling her to something more? She recognized that she needed to maintain her current employment to help support her family financially. And she recognized that she couldn't spend more time away from her young children. On the other hand, the spiritual fruitfulness she was encountering felt like a sign that God wanted her to continue to help these women, but she was at a loss regarding what God wanted her to do for their ongoing care. She was at a crossroads in her apostolate and had no one to guide her in understanding and discerning her call.

Several weeks after hearing this lay apostle's story I began to contemplate what would happen in our parish communities if we had more lay men and women like her. How would we nurture and support them and the fruits of their work? The vast majority of our pastoral practices make no room for individuals like her, and yet what she was experiencing was the normal life of discipleship.

When I shared her story with several national diocesan leaders, they were quick to canonize her and set her apart as someone who was an exception. They advised that she get a spiritual director because there was nothing more that could be done for her on the parish level. A spiritual director certainly would have benefited this lay apostle, but her spiritual needs were raising a broader and significantly more challenging issue. It was becoming clear from her experience that parish communities are not only challenged in welcoming those farthest from God but also that parishes are challenged in welcoming individuals who are beginning to live out their vocational call.

Individuals who are beginning to live out their vocational call challenge our parish communities because they point out the boundaries and confining limits we place on our understanding of ministry and vocation. What this lay apostle was encountering was the gap that exists between the Church's pastoral practice and its teachings. The Church teaches that the whole Church bears responsibility for the discernment of each individual's charisms and vocation. Not only that, but the whole Church bears responsibility for every man's and woman's vocation reaching its maturity (*Pastores Dabo Vobis*, 40). What we find instead in our parish communities is little or no support or formation for an individual discerning a vocation within the secular world as a layperson.

When God moves in the lives of his people, his movement tends to also involve raising up a means of sustaining and nurturing the grace that he gives. It is not enough for an individual or a group to simply prepare for and receive the graces God sends. It takes a whole community to support the work of God in an individual. The seeds of grace grow more easily in an environment that nurtures and sustains the seed in its cycle of life. From the preparation of the soil to planting the seed to the seed's germination and its growth and its maturity and production of fruit, every part of the development of grace in the life of individuals needs tending to.

The seeds of grace mature not only through the personal response of the individual who receives them, but much of the development and growth of these seeds are dependent on the communal environment that can hinder or enhance the personal response of an individual. An individual person grows in receptivity to God when surrounded by a community that collectively strives to care for the whole cycle of the life of grace.

Communal Spiritual Growth and the Big Three

If we want a parish community to care for the whole cycle of the life of grace, it will have to grow spiritually — not as isolated members but rather together, as a body. One of the central things we can learn from salvation history is that communities grow in stages. As a parish develops spiritually, its members grow in their collective understanding of their identity and mission. And so, if we are to cooperate with God in his work of renewing and transforming parish life, then we need to understand where a community is and where it needs to go.

Determining where a community is and its future direction is not something that is decided merely by the subjective observations of an individual or small group of parish leaders. Nor is the current state of the parish and its future direction defined solely on the perceived needs of the local neighborhood.

Understanding the current spiritual state of a parish community is not an invitation for the community to engage in self-referential reflection. Rather, it is an invitation for the parish to observe its pastoral practices and the spiritual needs of the local neighborhood through the eyes of Sacred Scripture and Tradition. Parish renewal can begin only when we can look upon the parish community and the needs of the people with the eyes of Jesus.

Pope Francis provides us with a beautiful starting place for parish renewal in *The Joy of the Gospel*. He writes:

> "The Church must look with penetrating eyes within herself, ponder the mystery of her own being.... This vivid and lively self-awareness inevitably leads to a comparison between the ideal image of the Church as Christ envisaged her and loved her as his holy and spotless bride (cf. Eph 5:27), and the actual image which the Church presents to the world today.... This is the source of the Church's heroic and impatient struggle for renewal: the struggle to correct those flaws introduced by her members which her own self-examination, mirroring her exemplar, Christ, points out to her and condemns." (26, quoting Blessed Pope Paul VI)

The actual image a parish presents to the world is what we might call a parish's culture. Every parish has a culture — it's who we are as a community. As with any culture, we can't label an entire group of people and say they are all one way, but we most certainly can say there are particular expressions, perspectives, and ways of living that are dominant traits and characteristics of a group of people. These characteristics and dominant traits are clues for uncovering the spiritual condition of parish life.

As we try to understand the pastoral realities of a parish, it's important to note that a parish's culture does not tell us — and never can tell us — where every individual is in his or her personal spiritual development. History stands as a witness to the fact that countless saints grew to the heights of sanctity in the midst of the most spiritually harsh environments.

We can and should, however, look at the traits of a community: its language and how it talks about God, its goals, its questions and concerns, what it perceives to be the spiritual needs of others, its sense of mission, what it regards as fruitful ministry, its structures and processes, how it uses its resources, how it describes the community, and what its engagement with the secular world is like. From there we can adequately discern what areas of parish life need renewal in order for it to better carry out its divine mission of making disciples.

It's difficult to make a journey without a clear destination. What is the destination — the overarching goal — of parishes as they cooperate with God in the work of renewal? Peter Maurin, co-founder of the Catholic Worker movement, offers a maxim that provides an entry point toward greater clarity. Peter was fond of saying, "We must make the kind of society where it is easier for people to be good." Apply this spiritual maxim to the ecclesial society of the parish and we get a clear picture of the type of culture we want to assist God in forming. The overarching goal of parish renewal is this: to create a community where it is easier for individuals to become intentional disciples, live as intentional disciples, and make intentional disciples.

Is our parish community a place where it is easy for someone to become and live as an intentional disciple, and to help make intentional disciples? What enables a parish culture to become a disciple-making culture? Where does a parish community begin when it wants to shape its culture to achieve the goal of making disciples?

In the 1980s, Pope St. John Paul II called for a new evangelization, and he gave us the critical elements — the Big Three — of a disciple-making culture. The new evangelization is not new in its content, which is always the proclamation of the Gospel of Jesus Christ, but it is new, he said, in its ardor, method, and expression. These three characteristics reveal where we need to focus our community's energy in order to transform the parish into a culture where discipleship is normative.

What would it look like if we took these characteristics of new ardor, method, and expression and shaped the culture of the parish to achieve the overarching goal of parish renewal? We would see a community focusing its communal energies in three ways.

First: New Ardor

A community would strive to instill in its members a strong passion to help others overcome the obstacles — the spiritual challenges — that prevent them from becoming disciples. The individuals in the community do this by listening carefully to the life experiences of others, determining where someone is along the journey to discipleship, and discerning the best means to help each person move further along on the journey. Disciples would be tireless in drawing individuals to Jesus by the divine power of the kerygma and in living a life that witnesses to the truths of the Gospel (cf. Doctrinal Note on Some Aspects of Evangelization, 8).

The Acts of the Apostles, chapter four, provides a clear image of a community filled with new ardor. Peter and John were put into custody for "proclaiming in Jesus the resurrection of the dead." When they were brought before the leaders, elders, and scribes, they were ordered "not to speak or teach at all in the name of Jesus" to which Peter and John respond, "It is impossible for us not to speak about what we have seen and heard" (Acts 4:2, 18, 20).

After being released, they shared with *their own people* what the elders and chief priests had told them. The response of the community was astonishing: "they raised their voices to God with one accord," the place they were gathered shook, "and they were all filled with the holy Spirit and continued to speak the word of God with boldness" (Acts 4:24, 31).

Second: New Method

A community would seek to create communal methods that facilitate and sustain the overarching goal of parish renewal. Communal methods are the disciple-making strategy the whole community owns, cares for, and supports as a top priority. From the pastor to staff, ministry leaders, and those involved or minimally involved in the life of the parish — each of them is given clear practical steps on how to promote, participate, and take ownership of the disciple-making process.

Four years ago one parish decided to create a communal method for reaching the unchurched and unbelieving. They chose a seven-week evangelizing experience. To introduce this communal method as part of a permanent first step in the parish's disciple-making process, they gathered together all of their ministry leaders, staff, and interested parishioners and presented the plan so that all would feel a sense of ownership and participation.

Next, prior to the main seven-week evangelizing experience, they presented to parishioners — over the course of three weeks — simple ways they could reach out to loved ones, neighbors, and coworkers who were unchurched and unbelieving. When the evangelization experience started, they were surprised to find that over 220 individuals had signed up and most of the participants were in fact unchurched and nonbelievers.

After four years of offering this seven-week experience once a year, over 600 individuals have participated in this communal method of evangelization. The impact on the parish's identity has been enormous, as this approach slowly moves the whole community to focus its energies and resources outward and is making the work of evangelization the work of all the baptized. It is also breaking down barriers that once existed between ministries and creating real opportunities for collaboration to take place. This parish is now discerning the next communal method that should be introduced to further form the community on how to live as disciples.

Third: New Expression

The community would work toward shaping its language, mentality, customs, and behaviors to make disciples. They would recognize how ecclesial culture impacts individuals who feel like outsiders in the parish community. They would also communicate clearly the demands of the Gospel.

Pope Francis, while speaking to the bishops of Brazil, touched on the importance of language. He said, "At times we lose people because they don't understand what we are saying, because we have forgotten the language of simplicity and import an intellectualism foreign to our people."[1]

The story of Pentecost provides us with a powerful symbol of reaching each person in his or her own language: the apostles preach in their own language, but the crowd, from many nations, understands. The effects of this experience opened the crowd

---

[1]   Pope Francis, Meeting with the Bishops of Brazil, World Youth Day, July 28, 2013.

to hear Peter proclaim the Gospel message. We need to reach people where they are in their relationship with God. The only way we can do that is by speaking in a language that is familiar and compelling to them.

* * *

In order to build a culture of discipleship and to bear long-lasting fruit, the parish must develop, facilitate, and sustain each of these three areas simultaneously. Jesus asked his followers not merely to bear fruit but to "bear fruit that will remain" (John 15:16). This demands our stewardship if we are to sustain the spiritual fruit God wants to produce through us. This is precisely the reason we were chosen and appointed in the first place — to bear fruit that will remain! Yet in our pastoral practice, we can tend to focus on only one or two areas of the new evangelization rather than on all three. The result? Limited, or poorly sustained, or *no* spiritual fruit. In order to form long-lasting fruit that is evident in the spiritual growth of the individual and the community, we must care for all three areas.

When we focus only on new ardor, we end up with individuals who encounter Jesus and become disciples but have no visible community to support them. Without ecclesial structures that are "owned" and recognized by the whole community, the work of evangelization becomes compartmentalized, something cared for by a few people. Evangelization, siloed, becomes "just another ministry" the parish does. Communities that have evangelization retreats or evangelization teams that are divorced from the whole of parish life frequently experience this stunted growth. Their evangelizing experiences yield fruits of conversion and the release of baptismal grace, but the small fire they have stirred up has no way to sustain itself without a community to support it.

When we focus on new method alone, we merely adjust our parish programs and structures but fail to center on or impact an individual's personal relationship with Jesus. A parish that approaches its transformation from this standpoint isn't really developing an evangelistic approach centered on discipleship; it's trying to answer the challenges merely by doing things differently. As Pope Francis cautions in *The Joy of the Gospel*:

> There are ecclesial structures which can hamper efforts at evangelization, yet even good structures are only helpful when there is a life constantly driving, sustaining and assessing them. Without new life and an authentic evangelical spirit, without the Church's "fidelity to her own calling," any new structure will soon prove ineffective. (26)

When we focus on new expressions alone — and this is perhaps the most deceiving hazard — we can find that our community is talking about evangelization and discipleship but is taking no long-term action. Discipleship simply becomes something we think and talk about, not something actually transforming people or the way we do things.

MOVING FROM HERE TO THERE

Several years ago my family sought to do the impossible. We decided to move! As everyone who has a big family knows, moving from one place to another is a huge operation. Often, as I struggled with the details of our move, I found myself contemplating the biblical story of the Exodus. This gave me comfort because it occurred to me that I had a much easier task than Moses. I had to move a family from one place to another, but Moses had to move a whole nation.

I began to think about what it was like to have an entire nation pack its bags, gather its livestock, and begin the journey: "The Israelites set out from Rameses for Succoth, about six hundred thousand men on foot, not counting the children. A crowd of mixed ancestry also went up with them, with livestock in great abundance, both flocks and herds" (Exodus 12:37-38).

Moving a nation sounds like an impossible task, but these two little details nearly pushed me over the edge: "*[The Israelites] asked the Egyptians for articles of silver and gold and for clothing.... [T]hey let them have whatever they asked for*" (Exodus 12:35, 36, emphasis added). So the Israelites not only were carrying their own belongs, but they also decided to take the Egyptians' items as well. But wait, there's still more. Scripture also says, "*They did not even prepare food for the journey*" (Exodus 12:39, emphasis added).

Exodus tells the story of a people who had to be on the move and who, in the process, found that their communal identity and the way they related to God as a people were forever changed. The journey a parish community must make in order to be renewed is similar. The parish needs to move from one place to another — from their current parish culture to another — and this renewal process will happen again and again. Like the exodus of the Jews from Egypt to the Promised Land, the transformation of a community — both internally and externally — can be done only by the grace of God.

So where are we as a parish? What are some of the characteristics of our current parish culture? More important, where are we going? What are the characteristics of a parish culture that makes disciples?

A parish needs to move from being a maintenance-driven community to being a mission-oriented community. In my work in evangelization at an archdiocesan level, regional level, and parish level, I have found that most parish cultures possess

certain recurring characteristics that earmark them as maintenance-driven. While it might be an overstatement to say that
all parishes have all of these maintenance-driven characteristics, I have yet to find a parish that doesn't have at least one
embedded in its makeup and identity as a community. Having
just one or a few of these maintenance-driven characteristics is
a sign that a parish still has work to do in becoming mission-
orientated.

Let's look at the characteristics of a maintenance-driven
parish and contrast them with a mission-oriented one.

Characteristics of a Maintenance-Driven Parish

The parish, fragmented into a community of communities, has
many programs and rarely talks about its communal identity.
Pastoral practice in a maintenance-driven parish focuses energy,
time, and resources on:

1. Getting parishioners involved in the many events, activities,
   and experiences of the parish.

2. Recruiting and training individuals to take on leadership
   roles.

3. Getting parishioners to commit to different tasks that
   would have them give more time, talent, and treasure to the
   parish.

4. Sustaining the current structures of the parish, thereby
   maintaining the number of people in the parish.

5. Relying solely on catechesis as the means of transmitting
   the faith.

6. Sustaining the inward life of the parish by providing formation for ministries exercised only for the parish (for example, parish catechist, lector, extraordinary minister of Holy Communion).

7. Communicating parish events and experiences with language that only "parish insiders" would understand.

In contrast, here are the signs of a community that is mission-driven.

Characteristics of a Mission-Driven Parish

The parish is diverse in its makeup but united in how it understands its communal identity. The parish has different evangelizing experiences that connect and relate to one another, creating a clear and simple path for individuals to become intentional disciples. This path is visible and the community understands that it has priority — all other experiences of the parish flow from this path or flow to it. The parish regularly talks about its communal identity as one that makes disciples.

Pastoral practice in a mission-driven parish focuses energy, time, and resources on:

1. Helping all people to encounter Jesus Christ and experience conversion through parish events and activities and also in life and events outside the parish.

2. Forming individuals in discerning their individual charisms and their God-given vocation.

3. Helping individuals to commit their entire life to Jesus and then to live out that commitment daily.

4. Sustaining a culture of discipleship, thereby nurturing and sustaining the work of conversion in individuals.

5. Transmitting the faith through pre-evangelization, the initial proclamation of the Gospel (kerygma), and catechesis in a systematic way within all of the parish events/activities.

6. Answering the outward call of the parish to the secular world by providing formation for individuals to take on parish ministries and equipping individuals to transform the secular world.

7. Communicating events and information with language that parish "insiders" and "outsiders" would understand and be welcomed and challenged by.

Pope Francis has a dream that we can make our own in our parish communities — a dream rooted in a desire to make the journey from being a maintenance-driven parish to a mission-driven parish:

> I dream of a "missionary option," that is, a missionary impulse capable of transforming everything, so that the Church's customs, ways of doing things, times and schedules, language and structures can be suitably channeled for the evangelization of today's world rather than for her self-preservation. The renewal of structures demanded by pastoral conversion can only be understood in this light: as part of an effort to make them more mission-oriented, to make ordinary pastoral activity on every level more inclusive and open, to inspire in pastoral workers a constant desire to go forth and in this way to elicit a positive response from all those

whom Jesus summons to friendship with himself. As John Paul II once said to the Bishops of Oceania: "All renewal in the Church must have mission as its goal if it is not to fall prey to a kind of ecclesial introversion." (*The Joy of the Gospel*, 27)

TRANSFORMATION BEGINS WITH A QUESTION

Questions have a spiritual power that can transform our destiny forever.

- "[W]ho do you say that I am?" (Mark 8:29)

- "Whom shall I send?" (Isaiah 6:8)

- "How can this be, since I have no relations with a man?" (Luke 1:34)

- "Do you reject Satan and all his works?"

- "Do you take this woman to be your wife?"

Questions have spiritual power because they can invoke a personal response. Questions have the power to transform because they create self-awareness and reflection. Questions carry the potential to form the minds and hearts of others. Just as questions have the power to transform the course of someone's life, they also have the power to change our parish culture. All pastoral planning starts with a question (*Omnes Christifideles*, 4, 9). No matter whether we are members of the parish staff or persons in the pew, if we want to help renew our parish we need to start by asking the right questions. What are those right questions?

We will never develop a missionary culture by asking maintenance questions. For the most part, that's what we've been doing as a Church, and it's one of the reasons we haven't developed the evangelical imagination necessary for reconstructing parish structures to focus outward and be mission-driven. We can't grow and develop an evangelizing imagination and evangelical creativity in the confines of "what we have always done" or by asking the same questions we have always asked.

If we want to make the new evangelization a reality, we need to begin by asking new questions. New evangelistically oriented questions and creative, imaginative solutions are beginning to emerge in the Church today, not simply because the Church is being exposed to new realities and is feeling the need to respond to them but because God is *asking us to cooperate with him* in creating new realities for our world, realities that we have yet to envision.

We can start the transformation of parish culture by continually raising these missionary questions for ourselves and for others:

1. How can we create the opportunities for individuals to encounter Jesus Christ and experience conversion through this event or activity?

2. How can we form individuals to discern their charisms or vocation?

3. How can we assist individuals to commit their entire life to Jesus?

4. How can we create a path to discipleship that is owned, supported, and sustained by the whole community?

5. How can we transmit the faith through pre-evangelization, the proclamation of the kerygma, and catechesis in a systematic way?

6. How do we form others in the task of transforming the secular world with the light of the Gospel?

7. How do we communicate an event or experience we are planning in a way that parish outsiders and insiders will understand and will feel welcomed and challenged by at the same time?

We can ask these questions in planning meetings, in prayer groups, in staff meetings, and at parish socials. These missionary questions will help uncover what the community knows and doesn't know, the next steps the community should take, and what type of formation is needed to move forward. These missionary questions will stretch your parish's imagination and creativity and help all to see their ministry and themselves in a new light. More importantly, if we ask these questions without assumptions and really listen to the answers people share, the parish will begin to dialogue about the things that make up a missionary culture.

So ask missionary questions! The missionary question you ask might just be the one that begins the process of transforming a parish community's spiritual destiny.

———

Bobby Vidal is the Director of Evangelization and Lay Formation for St. Kateri Tekakwitha Church in Santa Clarita, California. Drawing on nearly twenty years of parish-ministry experience, Bobby provides vision, spiritual formation, and direction to St. Kateri Church in order to help shape the parish culture so that the community might become one of intentional discipleship. Bobby and his wife, Shannon, have five children.

CHAPTER FIVE

A Parish Moves Ahead

Katherine Coolidge

Picture this: You're in your car, looking for the local Catholic church, and the voice on your GPS says, "You have arrived at your destination." You stop where you are at the corner of two busy streets. All you see is a host of evergreen trees and a wall upon which is written the name of the church. No driveway, no sign of a church anywhere. So, what do you do? You pick up your cell phone and dial the parish number. When the receptionist answers, you ask, "Where are you? I've arrived at the parish address but can't find the church!"

Prior to the fall of 2013, many who followed their GPS to one Southern California parish would do exactly that. Since then, the wall and trees are gone, replaced by stairs leading from the corner up to the new church, visible to all who pass by. A seven-year construction project left no part of the parish campus untouched: the new church building allowed for the conversion of the first church into its original, intended use as a parish activity center. The underground utilities were dug up and rerouted below a larger parking lot built to accommodate the growing parish. The result? The parish's reach and visibility were expanded beyond a core of active, faithful parishioners to anyone who came up the new stairs at the northwest corner of the parish campus.

The "before" and "after" corner images became an iconic representation of another, less visible, but much more profound transformation in the community. This physical evolution mirrored a change in how the parish saw itself. The parish church, no longer invisible behind a wall of rock and concrete fortified by rows of trees, presented a new orientation, toward the broader community. Serendipitously, mere months before the new church dedication, Cardinal Bergoglio would become Pope Francis and bring with him a vision of a church that "comes out of itself."

Rather than the story of how concrete and steel came together in a new building, this chapter captures the story of the people of the parish as they wrestled with something more complex than even a building project, and much more profound: becoming a community of intentional disciples.

To implement changes, large or small, in a parish is a delicate process. Anyone who has witnessed the debate that ensues when the flowers that have always been to the left of the altar suddenly are moved to the right of the altar, without consulting the sacristan and altar ministry, understands that change not executed well is often not received well. Navigating the waters of change takes humble, prayerful attention to God's presence in the community, knowledge of the fruit already present in the community, a visionary leader, and a willingness to involve many in the process. And, a providential moment in time doesn't hurt, either!

As it happened, Catherine of Siena Institute's Co-Directors Sherry Weddell and Father Michael Fones, O.P., were scheduled to present the annual parish mission on evangelization and discipleship. A number of key members of the parish attended the mission and were inspired by the prospect of becoming a parish of intentional disciples. At the invitation, and blessing, of the pastor, they formed an ad hoc evangelization committee tasked with researching and exploring this possibility more fully.

The fruit of this short-term committee would be to recommend bringing Catherine of Siena Institute staff back to speak to the parish staff and council. The Institute hosted a series of seminars delving more deeply into the information presented during the parish mission. Based upon the feedback of those who attended, they would present to the pastoral staff and council an evangelization strategy. This strategy would eventually give rise to a new mission statement and a new pastoral plan.

No Parish Is a Blank Slate

Although only fifty years old, the parish had a decades-long tradition of robust adult-education programming and well-established social-outreach ministries. Hundreds of parishioners attended a plethora of lectures, small-group offerings, and courses throughout the year. Hundreds of parishioners also engaged in some sort of outreach ministry on a regular basis. As with many parishes, there was a growing concern that many of the people coming were the same ones who had been part of these activities from the beginning. In short, the active members of the parish were aging and graying.

Thus, the first reality check for this newly formed committee was to recognize that the parish was not a blank slate and *neither were the people who comprised it.* Many in the parish gave countless hours and a portion of their resources in support of the parish and its activities. These faithful, longtime parishioners had a vested interest in the parish, and the success of any paradigm shift rested in part upon their ability to embrace and participate in future changes. And so the committee's next step was to engage key leaders within the parish in the larger conversation of what it means to be an intentional disciple, and why it should be integral to the parish and its mission.

WHO NEEDS TO GET IN ON THE GROUND FLOOR?

After the parish staff, the council, and the evangelization committee spent time wrestling with becoming a community of intentional disciples, the committee turned its attention to hosting a series of seminars targeted principally at parish leaders. The following summer a local team trained by the Catherine of Siena Institute conducted a weekend workshop covering the material now contained in *Forming Intentional Disciples: The Path to Knowing and Following Jesus.* (Since then, other parishes have used the book and study guide as another way to accomplish this same goal.)

Thirty-five people, many recommended by pastoral staff and council members, attended this workshop at the invitation of the pastor. In addition to leaders of particular ministries and members of the parish finance council, they included chairs of councils and boards dedicated to stewardship, social justice, and the parish school. Also included were parishioners with a charism for evangelism and RCIA team members, as well as key members and leaders of other parish groups and ministries. Members of the evangelization committee attended and participated as well.

For some who attended the workshop, the suggestion that it was possible to have a personal relationship with Jesus Christ was novel and provoked concerns such as: "This sounds too Protestant!" "Can a Catholic have a personal relationship with Christ?" "What about the sacraments?" "What about the Rosary and my other Marian devotions?" During one discussion, a longtime member of the parish rose to say that Catholics need only be told to: "Come to Mass, join a ministry, and keep the kids involved in the school or religious education."

This evoked an energetic conversation that would continue at various meetings and venues over the course of several months. At first, members of the committee were uncertain how best to respond and found the resistance discouraging. In time, the fruit came not from persuasive arguments on the part of committee or staff members but from God, in the form of chance, graced encounters in the life of the parish.

USE WHAT YOU HAVE

Intentionally including key leaders in these initial seminars spread the message quickly throughout the parish that it is possible for lay Catholics to have a personal relationship with Jesus Christ. This inspired a much broader conversation. Recognizing the real resistance they met at the workshop, members of the committee and pastoral staff were sensitive to the need to allow those already active in parish life to wrestle with this possibility themselves. Therefore, they first turned their attention to what already existed in the parish and envisioned how, within these already existing activities, small changes could help people encounter Christ in a more personal fashion. They focused on three parish efforts: current small communities, "The First 15," and a parish-based retreat process.

Small Communities

God had already placed in the hearts of many the desire to form community with one another. This could be seen in the number of small groups in the parish, some dating as far back as the 1970s, when the parish participated in a renewal program for the first time. With no prompting from parish leaders, these members of various small groups who had participated in the workshop began to share their own deepening personal relationship with Christ at small-group meetings. Parish leaders observed that, as one committee member stated, "With a little bit of elbow room, God showed up."

As they grew in their understanding of the thresholds — those identifiable stages on the way to full discipleship — and began to have threshold conversations with fellow small-group members, family members, and others, they realized not everyone is at the same point in their relationship with Christ. These testimonies and conversations fostered a sense of awareness and tolerance of one another's journey, especially toward parishioners with whom they were not well acquainted. Thus, the "culture of silence"— that reluctance among Catholics to speak personally about faith-related matters — began to crack as small groups entertained conversations about the possibility of a personal relationship with Christ.

"The First 15"

Several years earlier, the parish had adopted the "Question of the Week" concept, made popular by Bill Huebsch and the Whole Community Catechesis movement. The pastoral team adapted the concept and extended it into what they called "The First 15." This practice continues today. Each meeting at the parish begins by giving over to the Lord the first fifteen minutes for prayer and reflection on the coming Sunday readings. In this existing practice, the evangelization committee saw an opportunity to broaden the conversation without launching a new initiative. With some adjustments, the questions were revised to focus more on one's relationship with Christ and the challenge of following Jesus in the midst of his Church. As this format was already in use at all parish meetings, such as First Communion parent meetings, finance and pastoral council meetings, and pastoral staff meetings, the conversation spread far and wide in the parish community.

A good example of the impact of this small change was the experience of Sam and a small prayer group he led. Sam was skeptical, but since "Father said it was okay," he was willing to give it a try. With some reservations, the group went along with Father's request as long as, after one year, they could evaluate its use. After that year, the group reported that not only were they more comfortable sharing their stories with one another, they were also beginning to have profound conversations about their growing relationship with Jesus with other parishioners, friends, and family members.

This approach moved the conversation about discipleship out of the customary places of spiritual and faith formation into other dimensions of parish life. In the beginning, many were uncomfortable. Irene's reaction was typical of many: the first time she participated, she immediately turned to the pastor and asked for his explanation of what the Gospel passage meant. After several months, however, she shared how this practice changed her. Through it, she discovered a desire for daily prayer. Through her daily prayer, she discovered a desire to imitate Jesus and personally help someone in need, and found herself, in the midst of her prayer, asking Jesus to show her the way. The same day, she was asked if she could take Trudy, a woman without transportation, to Mass the next Sunday. She recalled her prayer and realized that Jesus had invited her to follow him in a very real way. She still takes Trudy to Mass, but their relationship has now blossomed and includes other outings than riding back and forth to church.

Parish-Based Retreats

Some years prior, the parish launched a series of annual evangelization retreats, hosting two weekend retreats each year: one for men, one for women. All members of the parish were encouraged to participate in these retreats held at an area retreat center to explore the possibility of a personal relationship with Christ. Parish leaders ensured that every parishioner received an invitation to attend a weekend. Over the course of six years, 300 parishioners participated in a renewal weekend, with over 200 of those attending staying on for a year of formation and preparation in order to present the next year's retreat.

Many of the alumni from the weekend would gather as a group periodically in order to stay in touch, as well as continue to grow in their renewed relationship with Christ. Others, expressing a sense of connection and investment in the parish, found a calling to various parish ministries or one of several leadership councils.

For many, the initial appeal was to find a place in a large parish that often felt impersonal. Some were new to the parish; others were seeking a new connection in the face of an empty nest, the loss of a job, or the loss of a spouse. Theresa was one such individual. Divorced, her children grown, and unemployed for the first time in decades, she moved to the parish a few weeks before the women's weekend that year. A faithful Catholic, she attended Mass but was looking for "more." Living with her dad, who was then in the early stages of Alzheimer's, she longed for a support group.

After attending the retreat, she found much more than that. She treasured her "parish sisters," as she called the women she came to know on the weekend. Her deepening relationship with Christ has become a place of stability and healing in her ever-changing relationship with her father. As her father's disease has progressed, her church family has supported her through prayer, respite, and meals. Through her daily prayer, she has come to the awareness that, as she put it, taking care of her dad is "my holy work, my work of love God calls me to do." The demands of his care leave her with little time, but she helps with hospitality after Mass once a month, and she now approaches her father's care with less resentment and more joy.

A New Church ... A New Pope ... A Renewed Vision

This shift within the parish mirrored the physical transformation occurring simultaneously on the campus. The new church, standing at the highest point of a peninsula, served not only as a visible reminder of the Catholic Church's presence in the community but also reminded the parish community that their mission field extended beyond those who mount the stairs to "come and see." When the pastor now dismisses the community to "Go and announce the Gospel of the Lord," those gathered at Mass face their mission field: the Los Angeles metropolis.

This shift is evident in the proposed evangelization strategy of the original committee, which became the foundation for the parish's new pastoral plan and mission statement: "Love God. Love all people. Make disciples."

This shift could also be seen in several grassroots initiatives:

- The team tasked with updating the parish pastoral plan devised a simple survey, asking respondents to name their hopes and dreams for the parish. They not only offered a paper version at Mass and parish gatherings but also provided it online. They purposefully opened the online version to the greater community, encouraging all, Catholic and non-Catholic, to participate. A column in the local newspaper, written by the pastor, encouraged everyone to go online and take the survey. Some members of the community did participate. A few came to the parish on Sunday to visit, sharing that it was the parish's openness to their opinion that sparked their curiosity and motivated them to come.

- Two parishioners with a gift for evangelization spearheaded an effort to raise the funds needed for a parish book giveaway at all the Easter Masses. *In the space of three weeks,* enough money was raised to give away 1,500 books.

- Inspired by the words of Pope Francis to "go out to the peripheries," a team launched a six-week series offering an opportunity to encounter the life and message of Jesus in the midst of his Church. One member was inspired to place a banner near a bus stop in a nearby town. Two persons came because of that banner. Not Catholic, they were surprised to be welcomed to participate in the six-week process with others. It became an opportunity for respectful dialogue with Christian non-Catholics, a new experience for some members of the team.

- As the new church was prepared for dedication, docents were trained to accompany visitors as they toured the church. In addition to information about various architectural and liturgical elements of the new church, they also received training in sharing their faith with those who came and information on where to direct visitors if they asked for further assistance. After the dedication, an open house took place for the wider community, and the docents led dozens of tours by appointment in the months following.

- *"Stairs allow visitors to come up ... and allow us to go out!"* These were the words of Scott to his fellow pastoral council members. Renewed in his relationship with God after attending a parish retreat, Scott found himself responding to the call to serve on the parish pastoral council one year later. At one council meeting, he proposed to the council that the parish rent a booth at the annual community street fair. They would be only the second congregation present at the street fair that year, and the only Catholic parish.

  Over the past two years, this booth has served as a bridge of trust with members of the wider community, Catholic and non-Catholic. People have begun attending Mass, and a few have returned to the Church because of the parish's presence at this community event.

With the publication of *Forming Intentional Disciples*, the material presented in the earlier workshops was now portable and more easily spread through the parish. Over one hundred copies found their way into the hands of parishioners. The pastoral council and committee that oversaw the adult-formation activities of the parish read it as part of their annual formation. The RCIA team read and discussed it as part of their regular meetings. As new efforts to engage those on the margins of the community emerged, key chapters were highlighted and discussed during the initial training sessions.

The book also found its way into the most unlikely of places. A member of one committee left his copy on the nightstand. His wife, Marion, picked it up and read it, cover to cover, in one sitting. She then called the parish office, asking to speak with a member of the staff as soon as possible. Due to the sense of urgency, the receptionist immediately called a member of the pastoral staff, who then called Marion from her car as she was returning to the parish. The staff member almost drove off the road when she heard this longtime, active member of the parish state: "I read this book and realize I am not even at the threshold of trust. What do I have to do to have a personal relationship with Jesus?" Fortunately, there was room on the upcoming retreat, which Marion attended, and she began a renewed journey as a disciple of Jesus in the midst of his Church.

What if Marion had had to wait a year to attend a retreat? Should she have to wait? As more of these stories emerged, various groups within the parish began to wrestle with how best to respond to the increasing need for parishioners and non-parishioners to grow in their personal relationship with God.

Small-group leaders for the various evangelization efforts and emerging small groups, recognizing the need to support people such as Marion, began to ask for training in how to help people move through the stages of conversion, how to talk about one's own relationship with Jesus, and how (through his life, death, and resurrection) Jesus saves us all. In response, the parish developed and implemented a short course that took, as its inspiration, St. Ananias of Damascus, who assisted Paul after his encounter with Jesus on the Damascus road. The course was advertised in the parish bulletin and on the parish website as open to anyone, but as particularly helpful for small-group leaders and RCIA and confirmation sponsors.

To the amazement of the presenters, the majority who showed up for the course were *not sponsors or small-group leaders*. Rather, they were ordinary people who wanted to share their faith with friends and family, or just have a meaningful conversation with a coworker. As those in attendance introduced themselves, they told stories of awkward moments, such as one person's tale of an almost-ruined holiday meal because his joy at his newfound relationship with God was not well received by the host. The change seen among the most active parishioners was beginning to spread throughout the parish.

As more parishioners began to probe their own relationship with Christ, the question arose, "How do I know what God is calling me to do?" With a pastor who shared regularly with the parishioners how he relied upon a prayerful discernment process when faced with parish and personal decisions, parishioners began to ask for a discernment tool to help them to know how God has gifted them for a unique work he has for them. The addition of a discernment process contributed to the growing realization of the diversity of gifts and call within the Christian community. Individuals felt free not only to say "yes" to requests for help but also to say "no" to others.

Lou, upon completing this discernment process, shared that "it is a relief to know what I *don't* have as well as what I may have!" Because of Lou's dedication, drive, and sunny disposition, he often was called to lead a parish ministry. However, he felt most uncomfortable out in front, leading a group. He much preferred the background. Recognizing the strong possibility that he did not have a charism of leadership but potentially the charisms of service and helps, he happily responded with a guilt-free "no" to the next invitation. Lou found that someone with whom he regularly partnered showed signs of a charism of leadership. The two teamed up to organize a large parish social event that offered the community a time to come together and celebrate in spite of a muddy parking lot and numerous construction delays.

Parish leaders realized a significant shift had happened in the parish. In the space of three years, the culture of silence had been shattered: not only did men and women believe it was possible for Catholics to have a personal relationship with God; they were sharing their newfound joy in Christ with others, as one put it, "at church, in the parking lot, and beyond"!

The work is not done. The parish continues to invite people to consider a personal relationship with Christ, to provide opportunities to discern one's gifts and calls, and to honor the living out of that call, not just in parish ministry but also at home, at work, and in the community.

As the stories in this chapter show, it takes prayer, consultation, and commitment to strive to become a community of intentional disciples, a vision set forth by Pope Francis, in which:

> All the baptized, whatever their position in the Church or their level of instruction in the faith, are agents of evangelization, and it would be insufficient to envisage a plan of evangelization to be carried out by professionals while the rest of the faithful would simply be passive recipients. The new evangelization calls for personal involvement on the part of each of the baptized. Every Christian is challenged, here and now, to be actively engaged in evangelization; indeed, anyone who has truly experienced God's saving love does not need much time or lengthy training to go out and proclaim that love. Every Christian is a missionary to the extent that he or she has encountered the love of God in Christ Jesus: we no longer say that we are "disciples" and "missionaries," but rather that we are always "missionary disciples." (*The Joy of the Gospel*, 120)

———

KATHERINE COOLIDGE is presently the *Called & Gifted* Coordinator for the Catherine of Siena Institute. Previously, she served as a pastoral associate to a suburban Los Angeles parish. Married to her husband, Michael, for thirty-four years, a mother to four and grandmother to six, she lives in San Pedro, California.

CHAPTER SIX

"Fireside Chats" and the Formation of the Laity: Bringing the Parish Together

Father Chas Canoy

In his apostolic exhortation, *The Joy of the Gospel*, Pope Francis stressed that "the new evangelization calls for personal involvement on the part of each of the baptized" (120). In order to achieve that goal, it's not enough that laypeople *understand* their vocation to be Christ's presence in the world, but they must also be *formed and equipped* to be those apostles in the world who will help people to encounter Christ and draw them into the life of the Church. Therefore, among the paramount pursuits of the parish is providing the necessary formation for the lay faithful to become intentional disciples and fulfill the new evangelization.

Pope Francis recognized, however, "that the call to review and renew our parishes has not yet sufficed ... to make them environments of living communion and participation, and to make them completely mission-oriented" (*The Joy of the Gospel*, 28). The problem is not new. St. John Paul the Great warned against the parish community seeming like "an accidental collection of Christians who happen to live in the same neighborhood."[1] Mary Ann Glendon, in her 2002 article "The Hour of the Laity," went so far as to say that the Church is "in the midst of a full-blown formation crisis."[2]

To place the formation vacuum for the lay faithful into context, I would like to use my last assignment as an illustration. My position was not at a parish but at a seminary, where I was part of the formation faculty. While this seminary also has a program for lay ecclesial ministry, the vast majority of its resources are invested in the formation of about 115 seminarians. There are ten resident priests, about another ten heads of administration, around fifty faculty members, and over fifty people on the support staff. It is truly wonderful that we invest that much in the formation of our future priests and realize its importance for the mission of the Church.

Contrast that flourishing situation in the seminary, however, with the resources of a typical parish. For the formation of over 2,000 households at my parish of St. John the Evangelist in Jackson, Michigan, we have only nine full-time employees, a few who work part-time, and the rest are volunteers. Granted, the formation of seminarians is much more intense, but can the leaders of the Church seriously ask and expect the lay faithful to fulfill the new evangelization out in the world if we are not willing to provide the proper formation that will equip them to do so?

While St. John Paul the Great may have sensed "that the moment has come to commit all of the Church's energies to a new evangelization and to the mission *ad gentes*" (*Redemptoris Missio*, 3), the Church has not yet sufficiently heeded his call. He knew that the heart of this formation crisis was at the parish

---

[1] Pope John Paul II, address to the bishops of the Ecclesiastical Provinces of Baltimore, Washington, Atlanta, and Miami on their *Ad Limina* visit, Rome (March 17, 1998), 4.

[2] Mary Ann Glendon, "The Hour of the Laity," *First Things*, November 2002.

level. Back in 1998, he highlighted the singular significance of the parish and its need for reform while speaking to a group of American bishops: "The parish will necessarily be the center of the new evangelization, and thus parish life must be renewed in all its dimensions."[3]

Where do a parish and its leaders even begin with such a formidable task as the formation and mobilization of the lay faithful for the new evangelization, particularly when many have yet even to be fully evangelized? Of course, prayer is the often-unsaid essential starting point. Even before I arrived at St. John the Evangelist Parish, I requested prayers from many people that the new evangelization would flourish there. I asked the nuns at a Carmelite monastery for their intercession. I asked that the staff join me in a novena of prayer for nine days before my first day. By summer's end, I had asked a team of about two dozen intercessors in our parish to lift up our evangelization efforts in prayer. As the psalmist said, "Unless the LORD builds the house, those who build it labor in vain" (Psalm 127:1, RSV).

Along with prayer, parish priests must realize that they cannot do the work of equipping their parishioners for the work of evangelization alone. It will require the valiant efforts of many laypeople, who, as Pope Emeritus Benedict XVI said, are "co-responsible for the being and action of the Church."[4] The realistic answer, however, does not lie in hiring more and more people to serve on the parish staff. Instead, it will rely on identifying those parishioners who will be, in the language

---

[3] Pope John Paul II, address to the bishops of the Ecclesiastical Provinces of Baltimore, Washington, Atlanta, and Miami on their *Ad Limina* visit, Rome (March 17, 1998), 4.

[4] Pope Benedict XVI, Opening of the Pastoral Convention of the Diocese of Rome on the Theme: "Church Membership and Pastoral Co-Responsibility," May 26, 2009.

popularized by Sherry Weddell, the intentional disciples who will partner with the clergy.

Put simply, it takes intentional disciples to make more disciples. Thus, among the first priorities of parish leadership in forwarding the work of the new evangelization is identifying those in the parish who already are intentional disciples. Only with these joint efforts and a shared vision can a parish adequately evangelize others and begin to develop the parish into that house of formation for the laity.

Now, how does one practically go about identifying and gathering together the intentional disciples in a given parish, particularly when many parishes have over a thousand households? There are a few imperfect clues that can at least help narrow down the search for those initial collaborators. Intentional disciples attend Mass regularly, of course, and one of the best indicators for Mass attendance is the data from the Sunday collections. Therefore, a list of those who donate to the church week after week is a good place to start narrowing down who your committed disciples might be.

Intentional disciples also place their gifts at the service of the Church. Therefore, another imperfect correlative of intentional discipleship is the parishioners who already are currently the most involved in the various ministries, volunteer groups, and service organizations of the parish. Just because they are actively involved, however, that does not mean they are intentional disciples. And so the next step is finding out more about where these parishioners are in their journey of faith. As Weddell reminds us, nothing gets at that journey of faith better than a good spiritual conversation in which the person is asked about his or her lived relationship with God. Though with so many in a given parish, how can one methodically begin such an endeavor?

"Fireside Chats"

There are many ways to go about this task of identifying and forming intentional disciples, but I would like to propose a way to break the ice with parishioners which is inspired by Pope Francis' refrain to look outward. This informal approach aims to pave the way for parish leaders to have more in-depth individual spiritual conversations in the future.

Upon arriving at my new assignment at St. John the Evangelist Parish in Jackson, Michigan, I addressed the congregation at all six weekend Masses to introduce myself as their new pastor. I said that I would be following the advice of Pope Francis, who encouraged priests to go out and "be shepherds with the smell of the sheep."

In striving to accomplish that, I said that I would not wait for everyone to come to church, but that I would visit parishioners in their neighborhoods and homes. After all, the majority of those listed on the parish's membership roster do not go to Mass every Sunday. With over 2,000 households in the parish, I recognized that they might wonder how such an endeavor is possible. Visiting them may take all nineteen years that my predecessor was pastor! So I told them that in my first year at the parish, I would dedicate myself to about two dozen evenings of what I called "fireside chats." These Thursday evening gatherings would be held in parishioners' homes in various neighborhoods all around Jackson.

Each parish household, then, either has received or will receive an invitation from me and someone who lives in their general neighborhood to one of these fireside chats. (We also recorded a video invitation that was emailed to each parishioner and posted on our website at www.stjohnjackson.org.) I wouldn't be coming to the chat with a long boring talk, I said, but was planning simply to "pop open a cold one" with them and spend time getting to know them. I asked them if they would share what they loved about Jackson and St. John, as well as what their future hopes were for both the parish and the school. The fireside chats would also give them the opportunity to discuss any questions of interest regarding our Catholic faith or how to grow in their relationship with Christ.

News of this novel idea of the new pastor having fireside chats in various homes of parishioners spread, well, like wildfire. Jackson is not a large city and is historically Catholic, and many people know one another. People reported overhearing conversations about the neighborhood gatherings at the health club, at graduation parties, at the theater, and even at the other parish across town. "Have you heard about Father Chas' fireside chats?" The local paper called out of the blue to do an interview for a feature article. By the first few weeks, we had over twenty people volunteer to host the neighborhood gatherings; I didn't have to ask individual parishioners personally to open their homes.

The fireside chats were accomplishing what I had hoped — fostering trust and curiosity. In her book, Sherry talks about the five thresholds of conversion: (1) initial trust, (2) spiritual curiosity, (3) spiritual openness, (4) spiritual seeking, and finally (5) intentional discipleship. When ministering to an entire body of people and becoming a parish of intentional disciples, parish leaders need to be mindful not only of accompanying individual people along these thresholds of conversion but also of advancing *the parish at-large* to being a community that trusts and is spiritually curious and one that is open and seeking. In so doing, not just individual people but the very culture of the parish fosters intentional discipleship. These fireside chats are one small way of helping foster that culture not only in the church campus itself but amidst the parish's neighborhoods as well.

This first year of fireside chats is giving me the opportunity to take the spiritual pulse of the parish and giving our parish leaders a considerable list of people with whom to have separate, in-depth spiritual conversations throughout the year. There are three other specific aims that I hope the evenings will help to accomplish:

- The first is to foster trust and solidarity between the pastor and the parishioners so that the pastor indeed is one with "the smell of the sheep."

- A second aim is for parishioners to connect with one another. Many do not even know how many people in their neighborhood belong to the same parish. This also provides an avenue for those parishioners who do not yet go to Mass regularly to interact with those who do. Active parishioners in turn can then help cultivate that trust and curiosity in them.

- The third aim is precisely that fundamental priority of identifying more of those intentional disciples who are willing to partner with the parish leaders to provide the necessary formation for the lay faithful to be those secular apostles, that is, those who are sent into the world to proclaim and live the Good News.

The further hope is that the fireside chats will not just be a "one-and-done" reality, but that they will help serve as a catalyst for neighborhood gatherings to occur organically. While it would be ideal if priests were willing to make such pastoral visits a regular part of their ministry, there is great value in having neighborhood gatherings without the involvement of clergy. Such neighborhood gatherings, for example, can provide a forum for non-Catholic friends and acquaintances who have expressed interest in matters of faith to discover and be exposed to more of the Christian life without having to enter into the RCIA. The Rite of Christian Initiation of Adults can be too big a step to expect some people to take, particularly if they are at the preliminary stages of trust and curiosity. Friendly gatherings where matters of the faith are discussed can fill the gap.

The organization and the detailed planning of these fireside chats were more complicated than we originally had thought. If every parish household were to receive an invitation to a gathering near them, to which home would each of them be invited? While there are various ways this could be determined, we followed these four major steps:

1. Using the parish database, plot all the parish households on a map.

2. Divide the territory into neighborhoods, so that each neighborhood roughly has the same number of households.

3. Choose homes in each neighborhood that will serve as hosts of the fireside chats.

4. Use age groups to narrow down the number of invites for each home.

In the case of St. John the Evangelist, we divided our parish constituency of about 2,000 households into twelve different neighborhoods. There are various software programs that can help you easily plot your parish households. We used MissionInsite to interface with our ParishSOFT database of parishioners.

The next step was determining the capacity of the homes that were volunteered and communicating with the hosts in planning the evening. In this instance, there certainly were more people invited than would fit in the homes if everyone were to show up. While one can plan for only a fraction to show up on the given night, there are evenings when the response is beyond what the home can hold. Therefore, to avoid disgruntled parishioners, it is very important to make clear that, while the whole neighborhood is invited, the guests are limited by the capacity of the given host's home. Such a clarification also encourages people to RSVP promptly. If possible, another fireside chat could be scheduled to accommodate those parishioners who wanted to attend but for whom there was no room.

While goals are important for any endeavor, they should not revolve around numbers of people in attendance at this point. The focus should be on identifying and gathering the intentional disciples of your parish. They will most likely be the ones who want to help you in the evangelization and discipleship of the rest of the parish and the wider community. Although it certainly is more encouraging to have thirty rather than three attend a chat in a home, the significant step forward is that time is invested to "go fish." In the midst of the busy internal life of parish administration, simply setting those to-do items aside in order to cast our nets and "put out into the deep" is an accomplishment (cf. Luke 5:4). Trust that the Lord will provide in these early hours the laborers in the vineyard needed to begin growing the number of intentional disciples in the parish.

"Spiritual Accompaniment"

As more intentional disciples get involved, how can they help other parishioners become intentional disciples? The ways are as myriad as there are gifts and outlets for those gifts. According to Pope Francis, however, the Church should initiate everyone into a particular way of being involved and that is the way characterized as the "art of accompaniment." When we engage in "spiritual accompaniment," we walk with others in their journey of faith and lead the people in our lives "ever closer to God" by making "present the fragrance of Christ's closeness and his personal gaze." This involves the "art of listening," a docility to the Spirit, and "a pedagogy which will introduce people step by step to the full appropriation of the mystery."[5]

It seems that Pope Francis is advocating that each Christian be formed so as to know how to converse spiritually with others in a manner that honors the dignity and individuality of each person. People need to have their stories heard. To put it into *FID (Forming Intentional Disciples)* language, the silence has to be broken! As a priest, I encounter many parishioners who yearn to share their journeys of faith. I wish I could spend more time with them, hearing their joys and struggles, without having to attend to the rest of the day's meetings and obligations. It would be spiritual food for both the one sharing and me. What Pope Francis recognizes is that this listening and sharing is not something privy to a pastor-parishioner relationship. Such sharing is part and parcel of Christian community life and the relationships between the members of the Body of Christ. Initiating your parishioners into the practice of spiritual accompaniment will help facilitate that.

This art of accompaniment complements and really should involve the threshold conversations described in *Forming Intentional Disciples*, whereby one actively listens in order to sense at which threshold of conversion someone may be. As with threshold conversations, "genuine spiritual accompaniment

---

[5] Pope Francis, *The Joy of the Gospel (Evangelii Gaudium)*, 169, 170, and 171 (with the latter quotation from Pope John Paul II, *Ecclesia in Asia*.)

always begins and flourishes in the context of service to the mission of evangelization" (*The Joy of the Gospel*, 173).

Parish leaders consequently need to initiate their intentional disciples in the arts of holding threshold conversations and of spiritual accompaniment in some organized fashion. They will be the ones who will want to be part of a larger team to help "make disciples" (cf. Matthew 28:19). They will be the ones to help organize the events and opportunities by which the rest of the community can encounter Christ. They will be the ones to take the next step of receiving the proper formation needed to be coworkers with pastoral leaders in the work of the Gospel. Sometimes you do not even have to search for them because the Holy Spirit will move their hearts to express their willingness to help. It is important for parish leaders to have an ear for those willing coworkers. Those offers unfortunately often become missed opportunities because parish leaders do not exactly know how to put the giftedness of parishioners to use.

In whatever ways intentional disciples are made known to parish leaders, there should be a next step in place for them to receive the formation best suited for their stage of life, vocation, and gifts. Before that can happen, however, they need the opportunity to discover their gifts. Thus, helping them to begin discerning those gifts through a workshop like the Catherine of Siena Institute's *Called & Gifted* program is ideal. As parishioners discover their giftedness, parish leaders can help them envision the various ways they can use their gifts to build up the Kingdom of God.

Too often, however, parishes do not have the adequate pastoral structures either to help all their parishioners undergo such discernment and formation or to facilitate the spiritual accompaniment that Pope Francis promotes. The huge size of many of our parishes, moreover, has made them unwieldy and more prone to losing that sense of intimacy that comes with belonging to a closely connected community. And so Pope

Francis, echoing his predecessors, has encouraged seeing the parish as a "community of communities" that "allows for true human relationships" (*The Joy of the Gospel*, 28, and *Ecclesia in America*, 41).

STRUCTURING THE PARISH TO
FOSTER INTENTIONAL DISCIPLESHIP

St. John Paul the Great recognized these deficiencies in our parishes' infrastructure. In his apostolic exhortation on Christ's lay faithful, he exhorted local ecclesial leaders to foster two specific remedies in their parishes:

> *a)* adaptation of parish structures according to the full flexibility granted by canon law, especially in promoting participation by the lay faithful in pastoral responsibilities; *b)* small, basic or so-called "living" communities, where the faithful can communicate the Word of God and express it in service and love to one another. (*Christifideles Laici*, 26)

These two recommendations signal the paradigmatic change necessary in the typical parish. The first recommendation of increased participation of more lay faithful in pastoral responsibilities addresses the current problem of not having the necessary number of laypeople involved to sustain the formation of all the baptized. The second recommendation provides the forum by which relationships of spiritual accompaniment can begin to flourish.

What then would a parish infrastructure look like if it allowed for more "participation by the lay faithful in pastoral responsibilities"? Again, it does not necessarily mean more people on the paid parish staff. It does, however, necessarily entail the methodical involvement of many intentional disciples. The Church has made very clear that discipleship and the work of the apostolate is not something optional for the mature Christian. Such duties are part and parcel of their vocation.

The thesis work for my Licentiate in Sacred Theology (S.T.L.) involved looking at the methodologies of groups in the Church known as ecclesial movements. Since the Second Vatican Council, these movements have provided much life to Catholic communities, particularly in Europe, where there have been dramatic decreases in church attendance. They include groups such as the Catholic charismatic movement, Communion and Liberation, Focolare, and the Neocatechumenal Way, which vary widely in spirituality.

One thing common to them all, however, is significant lay involvement in the formation of their members. Lay leaders have official functions within the life of the community, guiding specialized groups based on factors such as age, sex, vocation, and place of residence. Members invest themselves in small groups or basic communities that provide an arena in which they can share their faith and live it out in love for another.

These elements are the very things that recent popes have recommended to parishes. In an address to the Pastoral Convention of the Diocese of Rome, Pope Benedict XVI said:

> It is necessary to improve pastoral structures in such a way that the co-responsibility of all the members of the People of God in their entirety is gradually promoted, with respect for vocations and for the respective roles of the consecrated and of lay people. This demands a change in mindset, particularly concerning lay people.[6]

---

[6] Pope Benedict XVI, Opening of the Pastoral Convention of the Diocese of Rome on the Theme: "Church Membership and Pastoral Co-Responsibility," May 26, 2009.

And so we return to our question, "What would such an improved pastoral structure look like?" There is no one answer because the particular pastoral needs of a given people will inform that pastoral structure. It does help to consider various conceptions, however, and here I offer as one example the restructuring we have begun at St. John the Evangelist Parish, which has been influenced by the practices of various ecclesial movements.

Now, this is where the partnership of intentional disciples is pivotal. Using the data from the parish database and the same mapping technology as mentioned above, we had already identified Catholics who were regularly practicing and the neighborhood in which they resided. Using fireside chats, gatherings with existing parish groups, and spiritual conversations with individuals, we are taking this entire first year to discover which among those intentional disciples want to reach out to the people in their neighborhood.

In year two, we will gather these interested intentional disciples in each of the twelve neighborhoods. In essence, there will be another round of fireside chats, except this time there will be personal invitations to those specific people interested in fostering a culture of intentional discipleship in the parish and reaching out to their neighbors who currently are not practicing the faith. These initial participants will undergo formation to develop further that art of spiritual conversation and accompaniment that will help others move through the thresholds of conversion. For those interested, a small faith community could be formed in a given neighborhood among the intentional disciples of that area. A small team of people striving to build a sense of communion among sixty potential households is much more realistic than trying to accomplish the same for over 2,000 households.

Who will these intentional disciples spiritually accompany, and how will they make the initial contact with them? This question reveals to what extent a parish is willing to build a culture of intentional discipleship. Such a parish does not merely leave parishioners to create opportunities for spiritual conversations themselves but should be willing to structure the parish so as to foster and facilitate those spiritual conversations among its members. Such a parish empowers its parishioners to do so. Ideally, everyone should have the opportunity, should they desire, to be able to discuss their life of faith with another parishioner.

How can a parish begin to strive for such an ideal? We at St. John the Evangelist will be looking out for men and women in each of the twelve neighborhoods who have the gifts to be what I would call "parish representatives." All parishioners, depending on their neighborhood and age group, would be assigned a specific representative. These representatives would be among the ones willing to spiritually accompany the people of their neighborhood. They would be among the ones willing and eager to hear the stories of fellow parishioners. They would be among the ones willing to extend that personal invitation to parish gatherings, retreats, and formation events that will help parishioners advance in their life of faith and continual conversion. In sum, the incorporation of representatives into the parish is one very concrete and valuable way to respond to our recent pontiffs' call to involve more of the lay faithful in pastoral responsibilities.

Explaining and implementing the idea of parish representatives in the parish in a way that respects the freedom of each parishioner is critical. The parishioners' respective representatives do not in any way exercise any authority over them but are there to serve as a liaison or advocate of sorts for any pastoral or formational needs that parishioners may have. Having such a peer would contribute to a much more personal experience of the parish for each member.

There eventually would be a "core team" of these parish representatives for different age groups. Many of us are familiar with the idea of a core team ministering to the pastoral needs of our youth, but why limit core teams simply to youth groups? Why should there not be a core team or steering committee of parishioners who coordinate the unique pastoral needs of each age group? So, we segmented our parish population in the following way:

1. Seniors: 60 years old and above

2. Mid-lifers: 40-59 years old

3. Young Adults: 20 to 39 years old

4. Youth: Below 20 years old

Each of these age groups accounts for about 25 percent of the general American population.[7] The actual numbers at St. John the Evangelist Parish roughly reflect these estimates with about 1,000 to 1,500 people in each of the segments.

We hope that someone from each of the three adult age groups will serve as the representative for their neighborhood. Thus, in the pastoral structure at St. John the Evangelist of twelve neighborhoods with three adult age groups, there eventually would be a total of seventy-two parish representatives: thirty-six

---

[7]   According to the U.S. Census Bureau, these age groups accounted for the following percentage of the population in 2012, respectively: (1) 19 percent, (2) 27 percent, (3) 27 percent, and (4) 27 percent. Source: www.census.gov /population/age.

men and thirty-six women. We will leave it to the Holy Spirit as to whether or not the strategy will ever fully materialize. As we all know, plans change, but more important than the numbers here is the idea of providing a forum within the parochial structure by which the silence is broken and sinews between the members of Christ's Body begin to develop. As long as this is happening, then we'll simply allow the plans to evolve as the Spirit wills.

The "core team" for each age group, then, would plan and provide formational opportunities that would help their respective age group face the distinctive challenges common to their stage in life. Such core teams would be another constituent part of a pastoral structure — which could include, as well, a parish council — that promotes a greater participation of the lay faithful. They can serve as the necessary formation teams who work to prepare our lay faithful for the new evangelization and their specifically secular vocation in the world. They can be catalysts for the formation of small groups and recruit the necessary small-group facilitators. They also would be invaluable to the leadership of the parish, as their regular contact with the people in the pews would provide an important perspective on the spiritual pulse of parish life.

Segmenting the parish population by age, however, is only one way to help focus on the unique formational needs of the parishioners. There could be groups that help with different occupational fields such as health care and civil service, reviving the ancient idea of guilds. There already are parish groups that focus on specific ministerial needs such as marriage and family life and helping the poor. There are fraternal orders such as the Knights of Columbus. There are those groups that focus on particular spiritualities, such as the Secular Franciscans and the Charismatic Renewal. The idea is to have people connect within a smaller group of parishioners by which they can experience that sense of community and solidarity that is unique to Christ's disciples.

To sum up, calling forth these parish representatives, core-team members, and small-group leaders to join the lay leaders of existing parish organizations builds upon the foundation for a parish infrastructure that is more capable of providing the necessary formation of the lay faithful. These different levels of lay involvement in the areas of evangelization, discipleship, and formation provide the often-missing organizational framework by which to cultivate a parish of intentional disciples.

Intentional disciples realize, however, that this increased lay participation in parish life is not for its own sake but for preparing and mobilizing the lay faithful for the vocation that is properly theirs, that is, to be those secular apostles sent into the world to be "fishers of men" in their own right. A parish of intentional disciples, then, empowers its members to live and embody, in themselves, the very mystery that they celebrate on the altar — namely, the Body of Christ — and manifest that mystery to the world.

———

FATHER CHAS CANOY, a priest of the Diocese of Lansing, Michigan, was born in the Philippines and grew up in Missouri. He received a bachelor's degree in business from Indiana University, earned his Master of Divinity from Sacred Heart Seminary in Detroit in 2005, and completed his pontifical Licentiate in Sacred Theology (S.T.L.) in the New Evangelization in 2014. He is presently an adjunct faculty member at Sacred Heart Seminary and serves as the pastor of St. John the Evangelist in Jackson, Michigan.

CHAPTER SEVEN

Rethinking Youth Ministry

Jim Beckman

I was at the Saturday evening session of a teen retreat that we had spent months planning. This was the typical "powerhouse" moment of the weekend, and I expected teens to experience similar breakthroughs as I'd seen in previous years. But as I watched the young people around me, I could tell that something was not connecting. And if I was really honest with myself, I had seen this coming for a number of years. Our weekly youth-group nights, our semester retreats, the constant activity of the youth-ministry "machine" — it just didn't seem to be hitting on all cylinders as before. That Saturday night I watched as volunteer team members poured themselves out in skits, personal testimonies, and a passionate talk by one of the other youth ministers. But the crowd of teenagers seemed distant, as if they were watching something on TV, had grown tired of it, and were ready to change the channel.

What had we done wrong? Had we not planned enough? Were the skits not relevant enough? Maybe we picked the wrong speaker? A flood of questions ran through my head as the teens went off to recreation time after the evening session. Why was it so hard to get to the hearts of these kids? Deep down, though, I knew something bigger and more serious was going on.

Over the years, numerous "shifts" in the culture and in parish-based youth ministry have made the task of reaching teens more difficult: increased moral relativism among teens, increased confusion over basic questions about faith, the chaotic and busy lifestyles of teens and their families, and so forth. I had become frustrated and even disillusioned, feeling that I wasn't accomplishing what I hoped to. And if that retreat was any measure, I wasn't. We weren't connecting with the teens.

I do a lot of research in order to be "up" on teen culture, and it's clear to me that young people have changed dramatically over the years I've been involved in ministry. The "shifts" have been seismic, but the way I had been doing youth ministry had hardly changed at all in over twenty years. And it wasn't just me. I saw the same thing happening all over the country: the youth conferences, camps, programming resources, everything — they all had cosmetic changes from year-to-year but fundamentally were the same old thing just wrapped in different packaging.

I have talked with many youth ministers — one after another — who feel that the ministry they're doing is waning in effectiveness. They struggle to connect with teens, the teens seem to respond differently than they expect, and their ministry seems to lack "staying power" in the teens' lives, meaning beyond high school but often even just through the students' senior year. Many teens were unplugging from the ministry well before their junior or senior year.

I came to a conclusion: I had to change the way I do ministry. And I made it my goal from that point forward to be an advocate for change in the larger world of Catholic youth ministry.

Myths About Teens

You may be surprised that many "facts" we take for granted about young people are, in reality, myths. The following is by no stretch a comprehensive list, but it gets us started:

1. *Teens hate their parents.* Not exactly. In fact, studies show that high percentages of teens think very highly of their parents and want to spend more time with them.[1]

2. *Teens want, even need, to be completely independent of adults.* The reality is that a high percentage of teens have a strong desire to have adults present in their lives and have a deep need for those relationships to go beyond surface conversations. Recent studies have shown that one of the main reasons young adults are disengaging from their faith is because the Church and adults in the Church seem shallow to them.[2]

3. *Teens don't like church and are going to constantly rebel if you make them go.* No again. Three out of four young people consider themselves Christian, and modern teens are actually very receptive to faith, if they see it in their parents. The biggest shockwave from numerous studies is the plain fact that teens "mirror" their parents' faith to an astonishing degree. If teens don't like church, it might be because they see one of their parents not liking it, particularly their father.[3]

---

[1] http://www.childtrends.org/news/news-releases/most-teens-admire-their-parents-and-enjoy-spending-time-with-them-really/.

[2] https://www.barna.org/teens-next-gen-articles/528-six-reasons-young-christians-leave-church.

[3] http://www.ymtoday.com/articles/2664/the-national-study-of-youth-and-religion-in-a-nutshell.

4. *Teens are rebellious and increasing numbers are into sex, violence, drugs, and alcohol.* The truth is that the percentages of teens smoking, doing drugs, drinking alcohol, into violence, having sex, and engaging in other risky behavior is down, across the board in every area. And the percentages seem to keep dropping every year. Teens today, by and large, are good kids. Many researchers call them the "goody-goody" generation because of statistics like these. (It's important to note that although the stats reveal improvement, there are still too many teens showing at-risk behavior with substance abuse, promiscuity, and so on. My point: It's a *myth* that these percentages are getting worse and worse each year — in actuality they are much better than in previous years.)[4]

5. *Teens are immature and incapable of serious relationships.* The fact is, adults are immature and so busy pursuing their own stuff that they don't make time for young people in their lives, even their own children. The average teenager spends thirty-eight minutes a *week* in meaningful conversation with his or her parents, compared with almost 1,680 minutes watching television![5]

6. *Teens aren't capable of a serious faith decision — that will happen later when they're adults.* There's a common misconception that it's normal for teens to be indecisive and doubtful about faith, and to even leave the Church for a while. They'll come back when they get older, right?

---

[4] http://www.thesource4ym.com/youthculturewindow/article.aspx?ID=177, http://www.thesource4ym.com/youthculturewindow/article.aspx?printer friendly=true&ID=175.

[5] http://articles.orlandosentinel.com/1998-10-14/lifestyle/9810130534_1 _children-programming-rolie-polie-olie-quality-children.

There is clear data to support that this is just not true. First, most adults who are actively practicing their faith made a decision to do so before the age of thirteen![6] Second, teens and young adults who abandon their faith are not likely to return to it later. The data presented in *Forming Intentional Disciples* clearly demonstrates this reality.[7]

LET THEM EAT CAKE

The myths about Catholic youth ministry are just as concerning:

1. *Because teens hate their parents, Catholic youth ministry must offer an environment free from the presence of parents.* Yet study after study has conclusively shown that parents, hands down, have a far greater impact on the spiritual life and faith practice of their own children than any youth minister could ever hope to have. This is the case even for teens who get highly involved in youth-ministry efforts, mission trips, and short-term service experiences. In the long run, teens will mimic their parents' faith practice.

---

6 "Evangelism Is Most Effective Among Kids," *The Barna Group, Barna Update*, October 11, 2014: https://www.barna.org/barna-update/article/5 -barna-update/196-evangelism-is-most-effective-among-kids# .VGfJ0Ye2QnU. See also "The Development of Purpose During Adolescence," William Damon, Jenni Menon, and Kendall Cotton Bronk, *Stanford University Applied Developmental Science Journal*, 2003 (Vol. 7, No. 3), pp. 119-128, which highlights Erik Erikson's research about teens needing to commit themselves to a compelling purpose/cause/meaning of life or the result is purposelessness in their adult lives, which leads to many personal/ social problems.

7 Sherry A. Weddell, *Forming Intentional Disciples* (Huntington, IN: Our Sunday Visitor, 2012), pp. 34-39.

2. *Catholic youth ministry needs the participation of lots of young adult volunteers in order to effectively reach teens.* The reality is that many young adults are still fully immersed in youth culture and are frequently immature in their own faith. This can sometimes lead to issues if the young adult helpers start questioning their faith or abandon it altogether. I'm not saying that young adults can't be great leaders, but it is a myth that they are the only ones who can effectively reach teens, and it's directly connected to the myth that teens don't like being around adults.

3. *Mass and youth ministry need to be more entertaining in order to be engaging because teens don't like church. The presentation of the faith needs to be "slick" and relevant.* In truth, what we are seeing is that more and more young people are actually a little turned off by the slick, entertaining presentations. They want something real, something challenging and meaty. "We think they want cake, but they actually want steak and potatoes, and we keep giving them cake."[8]

4. *Because teens are incapable of serious relationships, youth ministry needs to overcome teens' natural "awkwardness" through fun, engaging, social events.* See point number 3; we just keep giving them cake.

5. *Because teens are incapable of serious faith decisions, catechesis — the teaching of the faith — needs to be done in fun, interactive, large-group events.* More cake!

---

[8]   http://www.cnn.com/2010/LIVING/08/27/almost.christian/.

Is It Working?

It's worth asking: Is it possible that conventional youth ministry, generally speaking, has bought into these myths and maybe even perpetuated them? Let's look at more myths about Catholic youth ministry:

Catholic Youth Ministry Is Thriving

The sobering reality is that only about 25 percent of U.S. parishes have really active youth ministry, and only half of those have hired a full-time youth minister to lead it. Those numbers don't reflect the fact that many of these youth ministers have to juggle additional responsibilities in the parish. And in the parishes that do have active youth ministry, fewer than 25 percent of the teens overall are involved. Not exactly healthy numbers.

Participation = Success

The Catholic Church does an excellent job of getting youth to come to events. We have millions of young people at World Youth Day events, tens of thousands at national events, and many more at local diocesan or regional events. And virtually every teen in local parishes goes through sacramental preparation for confirmation. When looked at through this lens, the Catholic Church has very high levels of teen participation in programs and events. And the main measuring stick that parishes seem to use when evaluating the success of their ministry is whether or not young people are "participating." But, as we know, participation does *not* equal a lifelong commitment to being a disciple of Jesus Christ.

Participation = Retention

It is assumed that if teens are involved in youth ministry, they will be well versed in Catholic belief, sort of through osmosis.

The National Study on Youth and Religion was a jarring wake-up call in this regard. It revealed dismal statistics for the number of young people who could articulately express what Catholics believe, even the very basic tenets of our faith. Unfortunately, Catholic teens scored dead last in every area of the study.

Serious Faith Practice Will Make Teens Religious Extremists

In a world marked by terrorism, it's understandable to be concerned about extremism. But extremism is not an expression of serious faith; it is in fact on the edges, the fringes. Serious faith is *rooted* faith, rooted in principles and beliefs that are bigger than the believer and expressed in healthy, mature commitment. This is something very different from extremism.

I can't count the number of parents over the years who have come to me very concerned that their kids were becoming Jesus Freaks. A little faith here and there is okay, but God forbid if they actually want to go to Mass more than just on Sunday. Or how about young girls who have a strong desire to change their wardrobe in favor of more modest dress, only to find themselves in serious conflict with their mothers, who are afraid they are becoming too holy. Again, the problem here is parents who have somewhere along the line detached from a serious practice of the faith themselves and are now threatened by the seriousness they are seeing in their own children.

A NEW DIRECTION

These myths all point to one central reality — the way we have been doing youth ministry for the past several decades needs to be rethought. And a simple re-packaging, or dressing up in different clothes, won't cut it. For ministry efforts today to be effective, the change needs to be equal to the seismic shift we have witnessed in the teens themselves.

In essence, if youth ministry is to succeed in helping teens embrace and mature in their faith, it must be oriented toward helping them become disciples of Jesus and fully engaged members of the Church.

The U.S. bishops fully support this direction in their document *Renewing the Vision*. In it, they identify three driving goals that define the aim of youth ministry:

- **Goal 1:** To empower young people to live as disciples of Jesus Christ in our world today.

- **Goal 2:** To draw young people to responsible participation in the life, mission, and work of the Catholic faith community.

- **Goal 3:** To foster the total personal and spiritual growth of each young person.

This provides a nice benchmark for what youth ministry should be — not necessarily what it currently is, but what it *should* be. And youth ministers — and parents of teens — looking for a working definition of "disciple" can find one in the *General Directory for Catechesis*:

The Christian faith is, above all, conversion to Jesus Christ, full and sincere adherence to his person and the decision to walk in his footsteps. Faith is a personal encounter with Jesus Christ making of oneself a disciple of him. This demands a permanent commitment to think like him, to judge like him and to live as he lived. In this way the believer unites himself to the community of disciples and appropriates the faith of the Church. (53)

DISCIPLESHIP-SHAPED MINISTRY

If that's a definition of a disciple, then what would ministry that actually helped young people to move in that direction look like? I call it "discipleship-shaped" ministry, and it's intentionally configured to move young people toward that goal. In order to do that, loving, caring adults — who come alongside parents in their concern for these young people — enter into mentoring relationships with teens.

As mentioned, youth ministry typically centers on large-group events that at some point break into smaller groups for discussion or other activities. This new approach *starts* with the small group, and then periodically — once a month or even quarterly — brings multiple small groups together for larger events. This decentralized youth ministry requires that many adults be involved in the formation of young people, not just one paid or volunteer youth minister.

You may be wondering if this is realistic. You may be looking for a silver bullet of sorts. Many people I talk with in different parishes are looking for a quick fix — a program they can put in place that will solve all their problems. I can't give you that. It doesn't exist. Yes, there are resources that can help you, but there is no one-size-fits-all remedy if you choose to go in the discipleship direction. Why? Because the work of discipleship is inherently individual and customized.

If there is anything I have learned after fifteen years of developing, doing, and training others to do this approach, it's that. I've led three different groups from their freshmen or sophomore year through graduation, and each group was radically different. The way I had to approach the teens, the things that motivated and inspired them, the ways I could get them talking and opening up, and so forth — all these were very different for each group.

Nevertheless, although the experiences in these small groups were radically different, I have learned over time that three common threads are essential to success. Although discipleship ministry is very individual and specific to the people you are working with, these core traits are like the "secret sauce" that makes it work. And so in your small-group environment you must:

1. Meet the basic needs of the teens.

2. Meet the basic needs of a growing disciple.

3. Stay true to the principles of discipleship.

Before moving to a few practical points, I want to break open these traits to help establish a foundation for effective discipleship ministry with teens. Practical tips for forming a discipleship-shaped approach will be useless unless we understand and are sympathetic to these traits and are willing to invest the time to walk with young people on their journey of faith. As disciples ourselves, evangelizing and discipling young people, we must be sensitive to their needs. As Pope Francis said in *The Joy of the Gospel*:

> An evangelizing community gets involved by word and deed in people's daily lives; it bridges distances.... An evangelizing community is also supportive, standing by people at every step of the way, no matter how difficult or lengthy this may prove to be. It is familiar with patient expectation and apostolic endurance.... (24)

> Often it is better simply to slow down, to put aside our eagerness in order to see and listen to others, to stop

rushing from one thing to another and to remain with
someone.... (46)

MEETING THE BASIC NEEDS OF TEENS

According to YDisciple, a discipleship-oriented ministry, there
are "five driving needs of teens":[9]

To Be Understood

Let's face it, adolescence is just plain difficult. Would anyone
like to go through puberty again? I don't think so. Between
hormonal surges, hair, acne, weight gain, and body odor to
emotional swings, fatigue, anxiety, and sexual desire — this is
a period of life marked by huge instability. Teens are struggling
to understand themselves through all this. They desperately
need strong people in their lives who accept them for who
they are and try to empathize with them. They're not kids
anymore, and though they're not yet adults they want to be
treated as if they are. The guiding principle for us as adults
should be: Teens don't care how much you know until they
know how much you care.

To Belong

This is straight from Maslow's hierarchy of needs. We all have
basic biological and safety needs, but we also have the need
to belong and for relationships. If we fail to meet this deep
need for teens, they're not going to be all that concerned with
understanding what Catholics believe and putting those beliefs
into practice. In fact, it's often the case that teens will succumb

---

[9]   See "Five Needs, One Solution," http://198.11.231.98/index.php/5-needs.

to peer pressure and compromise their morals and values in order to belong. Adults need to help teenagers build healthy, life-giving relationships with one another.

To Be Transparent

This is connected to the need to be understood. Teens are constantly asking themselves, "Am I lovable? Will I fit in? Do I have what it takes?" The only way they can find the answers to these questions is if they have a safe place to be real and transparent. They have a deep need to feel safe; that what they share will remain confidential; that they won't be judged or rejected. As they're able to be transparent, they get feedback from their peers and from loving adults and grow in self-awareness. Self-awareness is the foundation for personal and spiritual growth.

To Think Critically

Technology, social media, the ready availability of vast amounts of information, and consequent broad cultural shifts have impacted the way teens process information. They're not interested in answers to questions they're not asking. They're not interested in being taught, but they are interested in dialogue. They would much rather discuss, even sometimes debate, topics of faith and morals.

They need help developing their ability to evaluate, to move from the concrete thinking of childhood to the abstract thinking of adulthood, where they can wrestle with ideas such as love, justice, fairness, truth, and spirituality. They can ponder the transcendental questions in life like: How did I get here? Why am I here? Is there a God? Can I know him and his plan for my life? Good discussion questions geared to the teens in your group will help engage this type of critical thinking.

For Guidance

When teens themselves have been surveyed about the adults they look up to, not including their parents, a miniscule number name celebrities, sports figures, political figures, and so forth. They overwhelmingly name the adults who are nearest to them: relatives, teachers, coaches, pastors, youth ministers, and such. Adults are uniquely positioned to make a lasting impression on teens if they are equipped and given the opportunity to truly mentor them.

When it comes to the faith of teenagers, more is caught than taught. And this starts with their parents. Parents are the greatest source of validation and consolation in their lives, but other loving, caring adults play a critical role. The most effective way to hand on a vibrant and lasting faith to teenagers is through a partnership between parents and other adult mentors.

MEETING THE BASIC NEEDS OF A GROWING DISCIPLE

Basic human and social needs are uniquely met in the context of a small-group approach to ministry, but it's also important to meet the basic needs of teens as growing disciples:

Acceptance

This is similar to their need to belong, but in the context of their new faith-decision to follow Jesus Christ. On their path to discipleship, many teens will be leaving other friends, habits, and possibly even sinful patterns in their life. They need love and acceptance, and a sense of belonging to this new community that will support them.

Protection

New life is tender and fragile, and it needs to be nurtured and protected from bad habits, old paths, former friends, and similar threats. There is also the enemy to contend with, and that will be unfamiliar territory for most teens.

Fellowship

In my experience, most teens don't know how to be real friends. Many of them have never experienced true friendship. Helping teens get into authentic, virtuous friendships can be one of the most difficult aspects of discipleship-shaped ministry, but it will tap into a need that has been unmet for most of their life.

"Food"

New Christians feed on the Word of God, but most teens are not going to be able to do that unless we help them. We can teach them how to read Scripture, help them understand it, and show them that in Scripture we encounter Christ. Soon they will be able to feed themselves.

Training

Discipleship inherently involves discipline and deliberate practice. This is not something that will come naturally. The Church calls this "initiatory catechesis" and gives us three fundamental characteristics for this period of training: it is comprehensive and systematic; it provides basic and essential formation; it involves "apprenticeship" in Christian living.[10]

Mentoring

Training like that can't consist of information alone. It has to be modeled. I can't just teach a teen *about* prayer; I need to show

---

[10] *General Directory for Catechesis*, 67.

him how I pray and then help him start to try to pray himself. Over time, he is going to be able to pray on his own. This has to happen in every area of faith life. Teach, show, try, do — that's a true mentoring approach.

STAYING TRUE TO THE PRINCIPLES OF DISCIPLESHIP

And finally, I have found that there are underlying principles to effective discipleship that need to be honored:

Intimacy

Real discipleship requires depth and intimacy. As teens feel increasingly safe, they will open up. Most teens have not experienced discipleship-shaped intimacy — it's similar to transparency, above — so you'll have to help them navigate it in a healthy way.

Mutual Responsibility

Discipleship is dialogical, meaning "two." There's a transference that happens, from the discipler to the disciple. But it also requires the participation, effort, and receptivity of the disciple. This is a two-way endeavor.

Customization

Discipleship is unique to each and every person. It takes time to disciple, and the biggest share of that time is spent getting to know the individual person you are working with, and helping that person create a customized growth plan that fits his or her unique situation.

Accountability

Every disciple needs to be accountable to others for his actions, including teens. This involves sharing our lives — our struggles, our brokenness, our successes — with other disciples. In a culture that prizes isolation and radical independence, teens will struggle with true accountability. You will need to coach them, showing them healthy ways to express themselves in the context of your group.

WHAT NEXT?

All these elements are the foundation for discipleship-shaped ministry. If you understand the need to focus on helping teens toward discipleship and want to advance in that direction, the actual work of shifting to this model is relatively straightforward. You'll need a few prayerful, caring adult disciples who are willing to mentor teens and have the skills to interact positively with them (and their parents). Not everyone who volunteers will be a good fit, so be choosy. There are resources to help you find and train small-group leaders, but since you will be looking for adults who are themselves disciples or well on the way, you can also turn to *Forming Intentional Disciples* as a resource that will provide useful background information to help shape your "hiring" decisions.

Once these elements are in place, you simply start a small group consisting of six to eight teens and two adults (in any adult interaction with teens, two or more adults must always be present). Keeping in mind that you want to foster an environment in your small group that reflects the characteristics of discipleship, you start building relationships with the teens. How do you do that? Well, partially it involves the action of the Holy Spirit, but there are some practical resources geared to this goal.

I have found the material that YDisciple is producing to be some of the best.[11] I was involved in the early developmental

---

[11] http://www.YDisciple.org.

stages of this ministry and continue to do training for them. They are crafting small-group resources for discipleship-oriented ministry with teens that are specifically designed to meet their needs while giving the adults substantive material with which to shape a group. Everything you need to equip adults to meet with a small group of teens fifty-two weeks out of the year is delivered through an online platform — training materials, full video curriculum, small-group activities, and so forth.

There are also some great resources available at DiscipleshipYM.com, a new website devoted to sharing resources for discipleship-focused youth ministry, developed by youth ministers who are actually doing discipleship ministry in parish settings.

It's true that in some ways this is a more demanding approach to youth ministry, but I can honestly say that shifting to this approach has been one of the most rewarding experiences in all my years of youth work. Young people are coming to Jesus Christ and making the decision to walk in his footsteps. There is tremendous power in the small-group dynamic and the deep relationships that form over time. In the groups I led, we studied the Bible together, talked about the struggles going on in the lives of the teens, talked about their questions and their doubts, had fun together, and shared meals. All of the guys felt safe enough to share just about everything with one another. And all of those guys continued to stay plugged into the youth ministry programming that I was running for the whole parish. The new small group, however, quickly became the highlight of their involvement.

Being in intentional relationships with these young men allowed me to do far more than I could ever do in the youth-group setting. And as I got to know each of them, I also got to know their parents. Their parents would frequently host our meetings in their homes, and even provided food for us — which is always a plus with teens. As I connected with these families, I could see how my relationship with their sons was actually getting the parents more engaged. A number of times when a struggle came up for one of the teens, it led to a great conversation with the guy, his father, and me.

The fruit of this kind of intentional discipleship with young people is that well-formed disciples become amazing evangelizers. Discipleship is cyclical like that. The more young, authentic disciples you raise up, the more teens you are going to start reaching, because *they* start doing the reaching out to others. That's a primary aim of a discipleship approach — to get disciples caught up in, and actually contributing to, the apostolic mission.

But the fruit doesn't stop there. Where discipleship-shaped ministry has been implemented we have seen that:

- Teens respond well to the hospitality of adults and appreciate adults initiating genuine interest in them.

- When adults *personally* invest in teens, the teens stay engaged. Upperclassmen consistently stay involved, most of them until they graduate.

- Teens respond well to an adult mentor who loves them as they are, but who also loves them too much to leave them there.

- When we take the emphasis off slick and entertaining programing, adults become authentic witnesses of the faith simply by the way they are living their lives and being in relationship with the teens.

- Establishing brotherhood and sisterhood in a small-group setting empowers teens to have serious, life-giving relationships with their peers and the adults who genuinely care about and love them.

- A caring adult mentor, combined with a supportive group of peers who are all pursuing Christ, expand a young person's capacity for a serious faith decision.

- There is an increase in vocations among teens. In one parish, after four to five years of implementing this new approach, the parish had eight young men in the seminary and several young women pursuing religious orders.

- Adult leaders tend to be replenished with former teens who themselves were discipled through the ministry and therefore understood the method and value of this approach.

When we pursue discipleship-shaped youth ministry, we are getting to the heart of why we do youth ministry in the first place: to help young people encounter the love of God and become followers of Jesus Christ.

Since we ourselves have received so great a gift, we must do our best to help young people navigate these challenging years and to become disciples as well.

As Pope Francis has said:

It is not the same thing to have known Jesus as not to have known him, not the same thing to walk with him as to walk blindly, not the same thing to hear his word as not to know it, and not the same thing to contemplate him, to worship him, to find our peace in him, as not to.... We know well that with Jesus life becomes richer and that with him it is easier to find meaning in everything. (*The Joy of the Gospel*, 266)

JIM BECKMAN has provided leadership in youth ministry on the local, regional, and national levels for over twenty years. He has developed catechetical and youth-ministry training resources, is a nationally known speaker and trainer, and is a scholar in residence teaching leadership and evangelization for the Augustine Institute. He and his wife, Meg, have five children and live in Colorado.

QUESTIONS FOR DISCUSSION

Chapter One
The Generation of Saints

1. The French revival began when the reformers turned to prayer, penance, and a life of serious communal devotion and mission. How might these intentional-discipleship practices and perspectives impact discipleship today, both in your own life and that of your parish?

2. How did the "French School" of spirituality influence the revival? What elements of that spirituality do you see at work in the Church today? Do you experience the Holy Spirit leading your parish into deeper levels of discipleship and service?

3. Francis de Sales' *Introduction to the Devout Life* fueled a new respect for, and openness to, collaborating in mission with laity. Do you see a similar openness today in your own parish or ministry? How could you facilitate that attitude?

4. How are you inspired and energized by these extraordinary French disciple-friends? Who are the generation of saints?

Chapter Two
Praying It Forward:
Intercession and the Transformation of Your Parish

1. How has your parish experienced the "culture of silence" identified by Sherry Weddell in *Forming Intentional Disciples*? How have you experienced it in your own life?

2. What is intercessory prayer? Why is it essential to the life of a disciple? How does the mystery of "unanswered" prayer affect your understanding of and willingness to intercede?

3. How would you define a bold prayer warrior? Have you seen the prayer of such warriors make a difference in your parish? If so, in what ways? If not, why not?

4. What would it take for your parish to begin forming intercessors and intercessory prayer groups? What can you do to facilitate the work of that ministry?

Chapter Three
Co-Responsible for the Mission of Christ

1. What is the unique way in which the laity contributes to evangelization? How can you help your parish and fellow parishioners understand and embrace the role of the laity in evangelization?

2. Why is the experience of an encounter with the Risen Lord the essence of evangelization? How does the "culture of silence" directly impact that central truth and weaken the ability of a parish to form disciples?

3. Which of the strategies Father Fones suggests would you find most beneficial in re-imagining how a parish pastoral council functions?

4. In what ways would the "Apostles of Hope" model impact the ability of a parish to look outward?

5. What would be an effective tool for identifying those anonymous disciples of Jesus Christ in your parish who are attempting to apply their faith in their work?

Chapter Four
Intentional Disciples:
Bearing Spiritual Fruit That Sustains

1. How can your parish better support and form individuals discerning a vocation within the secular world as a layperson?

2. How would you describe your parish culture? Does the culture encourage parishioners to live as intentional disciples?

3. What are three ways a community can focus its communal energies to foster parish renewal?

4. After reflecting on the characteristics of a "maintenance-driven parish" in contrast to those of a "mission-driven parish," how would you assess your parish? What would it take to "move" the parish?

5. What are the seven missionary questions that can start the transformation of parish culture? Which of these are most pertinent to your parish situation at the moment?

Chapter Five
A Parish Moves Ahead

1. Is your parish community welcoming to visitors? What is your parish doing to identify and welcome new parishioners? What are you doing?

2. Change is a delicate process. What are some good practices for navigating the waters of change? If your parish is anticipating making significant changes, how will it prepare parishioners?

3. What can your parish do specifically to honor long-term, active parishioners and engage them in the move toward deeper discipleship?

4. How can this account of a parish's journey to become a community of intentional disciples guide your parish?

Chapter Six
"Fireside Chats" and the Formation of the Laity: Bringing the Parish Together

1. What is the essential, yet often unsaid, starting point of evangelization in the parish?

2. How could your parish go about identifying and forming intentional disciples?

3. Would your parish benefit from fireside chats? What would it take to get these started?

4. What are some ways to increase participation of the lay faithful in pastoral responsibilities?

5. Does your parish have parish representatives? What role do they play in parish life? Do they actively reach out to Catholics in their neighborhoods?

Chapter Seven
Rethinking Youth Ministry

1. Do you think that the youth ministry in your parish is effective? How is your parish measuring that effectiveness? Are young people staying with the youth group through high school or dropping out well before that?

2. Which of the six myths about young people do you find most surprising? How do the five myths about Catholic youth ministry impact your perception of effective youth ministry?

3. How does discipleship-shaped ministry differ from traditional youth ministry?

4. What goes into making the shift to discipleship-shaped ministry? How would your parish make the transition to discipleship-based youth ministry? What resources would you need?

5. What is the fruit of intentional discipleship with young people? Are there young people in your parish who are intentional disciples? How can their experience help your parish become open to discipleship-based youth ministry?

ABOUT THE EDITOR

SHERRY ANNE WEDDELL created the first charism-discernment process specifically designed for Catholics in 1993. She co-founded and serves as Co-Director of the Catherine of Siena Institute, an affiliated international ministry of the Western Dominican Province.

Sherry has developed numerous unique formation resources that are used around the world. She trains and leads an international team of teachers and trainers who have worked directly with over 100,000 ordained, religious, and lay Catholics in 130 dioceses on 5 continents. When not hanging around airports, Sherry enjoys tending her high-altitude Tuscan garden in the Colorado Rockies.